STAR WARS®

MYTHMAKING

BEHIND THE SCENES OF
ATTACK OF THE CLONES

STAR WARS®

MYTHMAKING

BEHIND THE SCENES OF *ATTACK OF THE CLONES*™

JODY DUNCAN

Ballantine Books New York
A Del Rey® Book
Published by The Ballantine Publishing Group

Copyright © 2002 by Lucasfilm Ltd. & ® or ™ where indicated.
All Rights Reserved. Used Under Authorization.

All rights reserved under International and Pan-American
Copyright Conventions. Published in the United States by The
Ballantine Publishing Group, a division of Random House, Inc.,
New York, and simultaneously in Canada by Random House of
Canada Limited, Toronto.

Del Rey is a registered trademark and the Del Rey colophon is
a trademark of Random House, Inc.

Library of Congress Catalog Card Number: 2002092098

Hardcover ISBN 0-345-43128-6
Paperback ISBN 0-345-45624-6

Manufactured in the United States of America
First Edition: November 2002
10 9 8 7 6 5 4 3 2 1

Lucasfilm Ltd.
Editor: Jonathan W. Rinzler
Art director: Iain R. Morris
Manager of image archives: Tina Mills
Image archives projects coordinator: Michelle Jouan

Del Rey
Senior editor: Steve Saffel
Director of production: Steve Palmer
Production editor: Colette Russen
Jacket: Dave Stevenson

David Kaestle, Inc.
Senior project designer: Rick DeMonico
Supervising art director: David Kaestle
Associate designers: Michael Gross & Lynda D'Amico

Original digital illustrations: Valerie Reckert
Stills photographers: Sue Adler, Lisa Tomasetti, Giles Westley,
Giles Hancock, Paul Tiller, Halina Krukowski & Keith Hamshere
Special thanks to: Rick McCallum, Lynne Hale,
Howard Roffman, Lucy Autrey Wilson, Sue Rostoni,
Fay David & Robert E. Barnes

www.starwars.com
www.starwarskids.com
www.delreydigital.com

BALLANTINE
BOOKS

DEL
REY

LUCAS
BOOKS

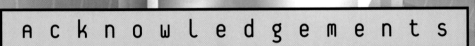

acknowledgements

The making of a movie is an intense, emotionally compelling, *difficult* endeavor, inevitably bonding the people involved as if they were survivors of a plane crash or a military action. The phrase *We feel like family* is as common on a movie set as *Let's do lunch*—and often as flip, because despite the bonding nature of the exercise of making a film, once production ends, most of these "families" dissolve, their members never seeing each other again, except perhaps from across the aisle at the Golden Globes or the Academy Awards.

The past five years, during which time I've been fortunate enough to cover the making of the first two films of the new *Star Wars* trilogy, I've discovered a *true* filmmaking family. Members of the *Star Wars*/Lucasfilm family return to the fold over and over again, largely out of a sense of inexorable loyalty to the clan. They treat each other well before production, during production, and long after production. There is a utopian sense of equality on the set, with the contribution of each member of the family valued similarly, regardless of his or her title.

Everyone lines up for lunch, and even George doesn't take "cuts." Everyone smiles and jokes a lot. Tantrums are unheard of.

I am grateful for being made a small part of that eminently functional family. Thanks to "cousins" Sue Rostoni for her cool head and warm heart; Jonathan Rinzler for picking up the ball and running with it; Iain Morris for shepherding the design process; Lynne Hale, Lucasfilm's director of publicity, for her spirit and sense of humor; and director of publishing, Lucy Autrey Wilson for giving me this gig of all gigs. Thanks to George Lucas, the benevolent father figure, for his thoughtful answers and his patience. Huge "thank-yous" to Rick McCallum, everyone's favorite uncle, for all the times he looked out for me and this book.

I am also extremely grateful to Don Shay, my mentor and friend, and to Steve Saffel, my editor at Del Rey, for their wise counsel and guidance.

—Jody Duncan

As always, to Caitlin and Larry, who protect me from the dark side.

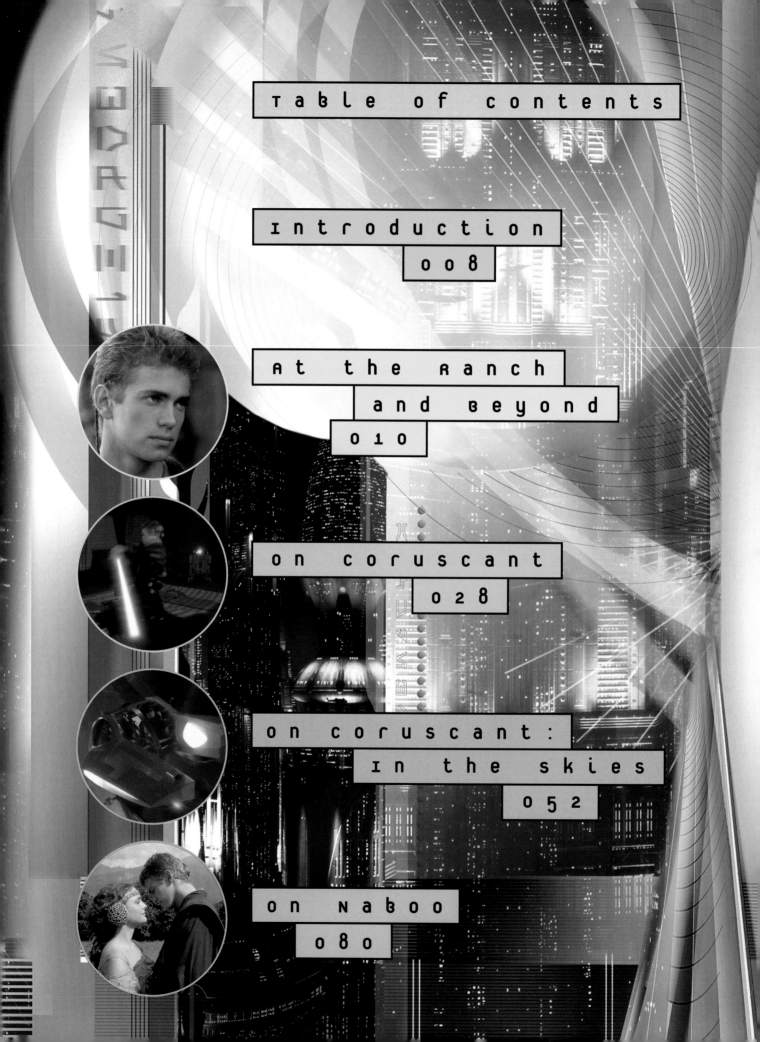

table of contents

> "It is easier to find men who will volunteer to die than to find those who are willing to endure pain with patience."
>
> —Julius Caesar

Introduction

The production of *Star Wars*: Episode II *Attack of the Clones* began less than a week after the release of Episode I. This time around, we had less time, less money, a new crew at Twentieth Century Fox Studios Australia, and a new Anakin. The script was late, set construction was late, and we were locked into a release date. We also had a brand new high-definition videotape camera, the 24-P.

As Episode II hit full stride, with our minimum thirty-six setups a day and sixty-seven sets to build, things were hectic. Over the years, I've developed a unique, if unfortunate, shorthand for gauging where I am in the production schedule: ten to fifteen pounds overweight means we've started shooting, while twenty to thirty pounds too much means we're in post-production. Just as I was about to upset my system with a mild case of cardiac arrest, everything began to fall into place: George finished an incredible script, dark and exciting; the paint dried just in time to film on Gavin Bocquet's sets; Trisha Biggar's awesome costumes

were finished in the early hours of the first day of shooting; our Australian crew surpassed our highest expectations; and Hayden Christensen convinced us all that not only was he good—he was bad.

And, despite many potential difficulties, our belief in Sony and Panavision paid off as their digital camera performed perfectly.

After two months of studio filming, we left Sydney to begin our location shooting in Italy, Tunisia, Spain, and England. The first challenge occurred as our overly tired, jet-lagged crew arrived at the Villa Balbaniello on Lake Como in torrential rain. But the downpour didn't stop us (we could always remove that later at ILM); in fact, the rain added atmosphere to the beautiful and tranquil setting, making the disturbing romance between Anakin and Padmé all the more real. We

carried on with our schedule, shooting the normal number of setups, and then moved on to Tunisia as planned.

In the Chott el Jerid, the desert dawn was as hot as expected. Although only George and Anthony Daniels had been there twenty-five years before, everyone was awed to arrive on the same exact ridge where Luke had stood and gazed into Tatooine's twin sunset. John

Williams's moving music soars at that moment and the film cuts to Luke's face, which clearly shows his fierce yearning to get out into the world and discover who he really is. That scene has become one of cinema's most treasured moments, so, as we set up the equipment, we were all determined to match that success with Episode II.

Following a brief stop in Spain—a single day of shooting that had required weeks of preparation—we brought the Australian crew to England, something that rarely happens. Usually productions take their crews to Australia, not the other way around.

After wrapping up principal photography and saying good-byes to the cast and crew, I only needed to look down at my growing waistline to know that we were about to start post-production: i.e., a race against the clock for the next year. Happily, we no longer treat effects houses as a separate part of the process, and Industrial Light & Magic (ILM) had been part of the production since day one. Visual effects supervisors John Knoll, Ben Snow, and Pablo Helman, along with animation director Rob Coleman, were already blazing along. Working hand-in-hand and pixel-in-pixel with concept design artists Erik Tiemens, Ryan Church, and Doug Chiang, as well as animatics supervisor Dan Gregoire, ILM was rapidly turning detailed animatics into incredible finished shots and replacing bluescreens with amazing digital backgrounds. Plus, characters who had been absent on the set were springing to life—most excitingly, a 100 percent computer-generated Yoda. In Count Dooku's hangar, lightsaber in three-fingered hand, he finally revealed himself as the most cosmic swordsman in the galaxy.

On April 8, 2002, ILM delivered the last shot and George signed off on it. On April 10, George and editor Ben Burtt delivered the final cut of the film complete with sound effects and John Williams's music. On that very same day, we invited hundreds of people to the Stag Theatre at Skywalker Sound to preview the film. For the first time many of the crew who had been working on the film for two to three years would finally see it from start to finish—would see Anakin racing on a swoop bike through a devilishly red desert landscape, would see two hundred Jedi igniting their lightsabers simultaneously, would see a fleet of assault ships with blue-flame exhaust thundering into the skies of Coruscant—and the excitement was palpable.

I was very happy (and relieved) that afterward, the buzz was good.

Today, although I've lost all that weight, the cycle is starting up again: Major casting for the conceptual art department and the animatics group is already finished for Episode III; George is busy writing the script (at least that's what he tells me!); sound stages are already booked at Fox Studios Australia; and Trisha is preparing to start making the costumes in November.

But Episode III will be another story.

Mythmaking is Jody's expert look into the story of how thousands of artists, craftspeople, and technicians—led by a pioneering director—created *Attack of the Clones.*

The myth begins on paper.

During preproduction, filming, and postproduction, the myth becomes visible through the work of hundreds of dedicated people.

Following the film's release, the myth becomes public and the public makes it its own.

— Rick McCallum

chapter
one

At the Ranch and Beyond

(T)he making of Star Wars: *Episode I* The Phantom Menace *had been an exhausting, all-consuming five-year ordeal for writer-director George Lucas; and so, soon after the movie's bally-hooed release in May 1999, Lucas left his headquarters at Skywalker Ranch in Nicasio, California, to spend two months in Europe with his family. But the movie that would become* Star Wars: *Episode II* Attack of the Clones *was never far from his thoughts. Even while vacationing, Lucas took note of possible locations; in quiet moments, he scribbled down ideas for the as-yet-unwritten screenplay.*

Work on Episode II began at the Ranch with (from left) concept design supervisor Doug Chiang, Lucas, and concept artist Iain McCaig.

remarkably, they found that the set was still standing. Approximately 170 miles from Tozeur, in a dry salt bed near the town of Matmata, McCallum and Bocquet inspected the troglodyte dwellings that had served as the Skywalker moisture farm homestead in the original *Star Wars*, an iconic location that would be revisited in Episode II. "We checked to make sure nothing had happened to those sunken dwellings," Gavin Bocquet commented. "They were still there and still usable; but we knew we'd have to rework them some, because they didn't look exactly as they had twenty-five years ago." To provide Lucas with ample reference, the scouting party took photographs and video footage of all the locations.

At the same time, McCallum was exploring production options in Sydney, Australia, where he and Lucas planned to shoot principal photography the following June—the first time a *Star Wars* production would be based outside England. One of the allures of shooting the movie Down Under was a new studio being developed there by Twentieth Century Fox. "We started looking at Sydney as a serious possibility," McCallum recalled, "and we eventually locked in a deal to shoot Episode II there. They'd just started transforming an area of old show grounds into a studio at that point, but they said they'd have it done by the time we needed it, and I trusted them." Between September and the

Producer Rick McCallum, too, spent that summer abroad, vacationing in between overseas openings of Episode I and conducting a series of "reccies"—or location scouts—with production designer Gavin Bocquet and other key personnel. Though they did not yet have a script or even a title for the new movie, members of the scouting team knew that the story would return to Naboo, partially realized in Episode I through locations in Italy. In addition to revisiting the palace in Caserta, which had served as Queen Amidala's palace in *The Phantom Menace*, McCallum and Bocquet scouted several lakeside locations in northern Italy, searching for a Naboo summer retreat that would be a pivotal setting in Episode II.

Because the new film would also return to Tatooine, the scouting party made another stop in Tunisia, where the Mos Espa set for *The Phantom Menace* had been built in the sand dunes surrounding Tozeur, and,

Nicasio

London

Sydney

(Left) Writer-director at work. (Right) Production designer Gavin Bocquet explains the layout of a set model to Lucas. Bocquet oversaw the design and construction of more than sixty sets for Attack of the Clones.

holiday season of 1999, McCallum made twelve trips to Sydney, traveling an exhausting ninety thousand air miles as he hired crew members and generally prepared the production.

Meanwhile, back at the Ranch, Lucas was working on the screenplay—as always, writing it out in longhand on lined notebook paper. "I sat down to write the screenplay in September," Lucas recalled, "starting on page one and working my way through a first draft as quickly as possible. As soon as that initial draft was done, I started right away on a second draft. I do a lot of drafts, rather than continually reworking the first twenty to thirty pages. I've found that if you keep trying to fix things, you rewrite the first thirty pages a hundred times, and you never get to the end. I called the first one typed up by my assistant my 'rough draft,' but I'd done fourteen or fifteen

Producer Rick McCallum, Lucas's collaborator in bringing the new Star Wars prequel trilogy to the screen.

drafts *before* that one, and I did another two or three before I had it typed up again."

Simultaneously, Lucas initiated his work with the Ranch concept design team, supervised at that time by concept design supervisor Doug Chiang. In the symbiotic approach that had served him well in the past, Lucas fed the design effort with developing script ideas and took inspiration for the script from the evolving designs. With principal photography scheduled to commence in June 2000, both the script and the designs had to be completed by May 2000, a period of only nine months from the September start. In contrast, the writing and concept phase for *The Phantom Menace* had consumed three years.

Just as it had been for the earlier film, the concept designers' mandate was to create distinctive, unmistakably *Star Wars* environments, hardware, and characters. "It took me a long time to realize that *Star Wars* is *not* a futuristic world," concept artist Iain McCaig admitted; "it is a mythological one. *Star Wars* happened a long time ago, so it is more mythology than science fiction. Consequently, what we design doesn't have to make scientific sense, but it must spark some recognition with a familiar mythological archetype.

"To create this *Star Wars* period, we look at a time of antiquity, like ancient Greece. What was that world like? Things were handmade. Little city-states fought with other city-states. That's exactly what happens in *Star Wars*. There are little empires fighting one another."

As always, the concept artists worked within the Main House at Skywalker Ranch, a serene environment surrounded

To illustrate the landscapes of prominent planets such as Geonosis, concept designers not only produced pen-and-ink sketches but also large-scale, full-color paintings. All artwork was scanned and loaded into art department computers to facilitate easy access and organization.

REVISED
GEONOSIS WAR ROOM
RYAN CHURCH
12 DEC 01
SW2

(Clockwise from middle-left opposite page) Concept design supervisor Erik Tiemens; concept painting of a Coruscant cityscape (Tiemens); concept design supervisor Ryan Church; the Senate on Coruscant (Tiemens); gunships on Geonosis (Church); painting of a Republic gunship (Tiemens); concept painting of a Geonosian interior hall (Church); the secret "war room" on Geonosis (Church); Padmé in the droid factory (Tiemens).

by windows and skylights to let in ample light, while providing inspirational views of the Ranch's undulating green hills. Large tables shared space with computer workstations and corkboards onto which were tacked dozens of concept drawings. On one wall, three clocks designated "Nicasio," "London," and "Sydney" were set at their respective times, a testament to the global nature of the production.

Lucas met with the fifteen-member concept design team nearly every Friday afternoon for nine months before filming began. "George didn't tell us exactly what the story was going to be," Doug Chiang recalled, "but he gave us a vague idea of the characters and environments. We knew there were going to be two new planets—Geonosis and Kamino—and so we started exploring textures and styles of architecture for those planets."

A t the Friday meetings, Lucas would review concept sketches and paintings, carrying with him an OK stamp, decisively applied to those designs that met with his approval. For the concept designers, the more OKs stamped on a piece of artwork, the better: one meant the design would most likely require more revisions and still might not find its way into the movie, while three meant Lucas loved the design as it was and definitely intended to use it in the film.

Concept model makers then translated approved sketches into three-dimensional models for Lucas's review. "The models were very important to the concept process," concept model maker John Goodson stated. "When we had our meetings with George, there would be all of this 2-D art on the table, and a few models—and where would he go immediately? To the models. He could pick them up and examine them from every angle, and that's why the models were so

useful to him." Working from a sketch of a vehicle, for example, the model makers would first build a small-scale, four to five-inch-long wooden or foam model to determine the basic three-dimensional form, then build a more detailed vacuformed plastic version measuring between fourteen and eighteen inches long.

Character models were sculpted out of "Super-Sculpey," a material that remains pliable until it is baked in a 175-degree oven. Because the art department wasn't equipped with an oven, the artists would take their sculptures down to the Main House kitchen for curing before and after its normal operating hours. Once baked and hardened, the fleshy pink–colored figures were painted.

The model makers also built miniature environments, particularly for settings in which complex action sequences would take place. An execution arena, for example—the site of a climactic showdown between Jedi Knights, alien beasts, and battle droids—was built as a five-by-three-foot model. Using little cutout figures to represent the various characters, Lucas choreographed much of the third-act battle sequence within that miniature.

T he designers produced more than a thousand drawings and dozens of maquettes and models by the time the concept phase was over. Each was photographed using a digital camera to create images that could be uploaded directly to a central database. There they were organized and maintained by art department supervisor Fay David. Once the images were in the computer, David could access them by type, date, or scene-by-scene chronology—the latter creating a kind of graphic novel of the movie that proved extremely useful in planning principal photography.

As crucial as the design work was to the development of the story, it demanded more and more of Lucas's attention as the months wore on, making it harder for him to carve out

Ishi Tib Costume — POWER 3/00   dp 225

process along. Even so, the final draft was not finished until the day before Lucas left for Sydney. "My assistant handed me that draft to proofread as I was getting on the airplane," Lucas commented, "just one week before I started shooting. Nobody on the crew had received a script yet. I had given them a rather detailed outline of what the scenes were so they'd know what sets and props we needed—but that was it."

017

T hroughout the nine months that Lucas was writing and designing and McCallum was tending to production matters, the imminent shoot occupied the lives of various department heads, such as casting director Robin Gurland, who spent the year filling all of the

the necessary time for writing the screenplay. "I would write three days a week and do design work two days a week," he explained. "Later, when the crunch came, I worked on Saturdays as well, writing four days a week. But even so, I had to work awfully hard and fast to get all the drafts finished in the amount of time I had."

Screenwriter Jonathan Hales, an alumnus of *The Young Indiana Jones Chronicles*, Lucasfilm's highly regarded television series, was brought on board to move the scriptwriting

film's major roles. No casting assignment for *Attack of the Clones* was more critical than that of finding an actor to portray twenty-year-old Anakin Skywalker. There had been much speculation in the media over the course of that year as to who would win the role, with well-known names such as Leonardo DiCaprio mentioned. Unknown names were also bandied about as possible Anakin "finds." Flurries of misinformation flew across the Internet, which were often picked up by the media and reported as fact.

ANNIE
REEK

RR   43c ✱

RR   44 ✱

Anakin wraps chain around Reek's horn.

RR   45 ✱

RR   46 ✱

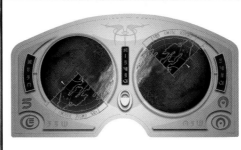

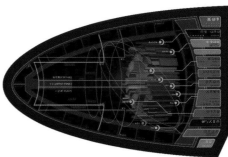

Included in the massive art department effort were storyboards for intricate action sequences (by Ed Natividad)—such as Anakin's rodeo-style ride upon a reek in the execution arena—the development of alien alphabets, and detailed schematics of hardware and environments by Gavin Bocquet's production team.

I 15 14 ⊕⊕
A   B   C   D
5 IE ⊖ ✳
E   F   G   H
4I ⊖ A E
I   J   K   L
5 ∃ ⊙ 5
M   N   O   P
⊙ R E 5 U
Q   R   S   T   U
λ λ ⟨ ⊻ S
V   W   X   Y   Z

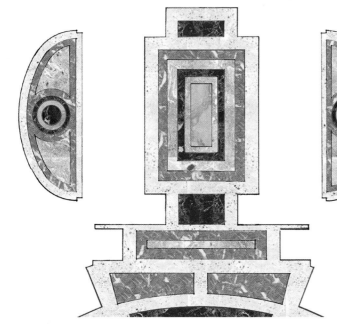

NABOO SUMMER HOUSE - FLOOR PATTERN w/ LIVING ROOM

FINAL COLOUR SCHEME - VERSION B

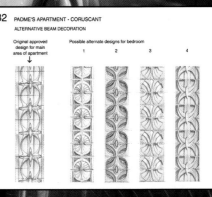

B2   PADME'S APARTMENT - CORUSCANT
     ALTERNATIVE BEAM DECORATION

Original approved design for main area of apartment   Possible alternate designs for bedroom
                                                    1   2   3   4

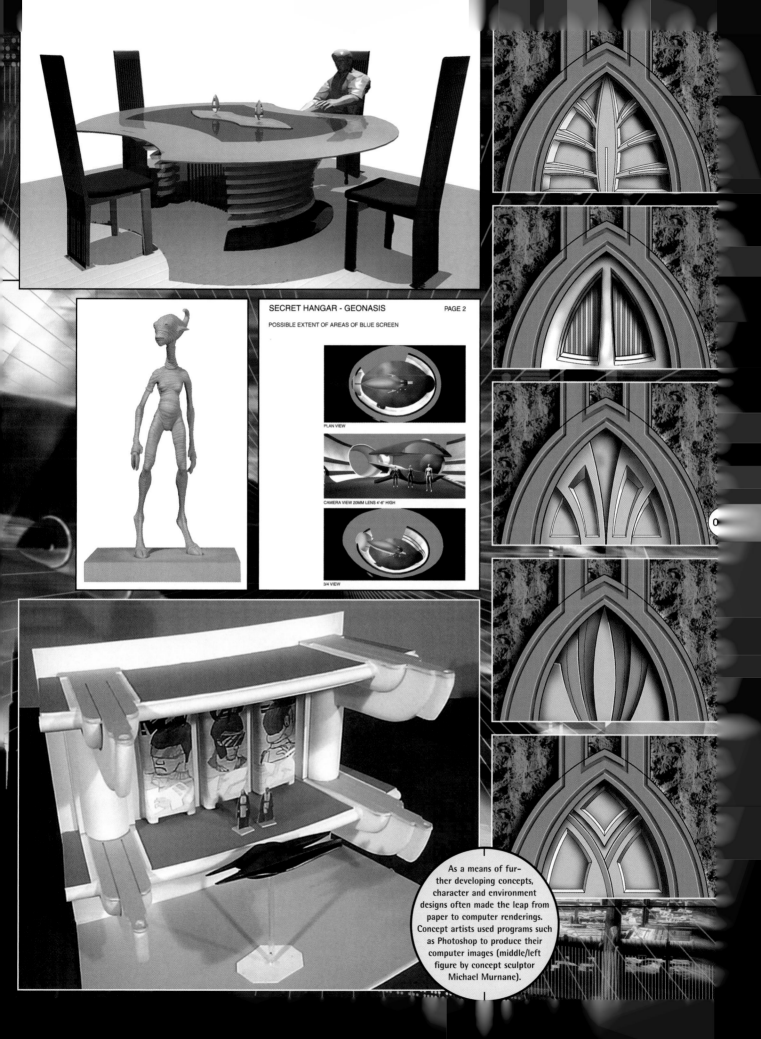

SECRET HANGAR - GEONASIS   PAGE 2

POSSIBLE EXTENT OF AREAS OF BLUE SCREEN

PLAN VIEW

CAMERA VIEW 20MM LENS 4'-6" HIGH

3/4 VIEW

As a means of further developing concepts, character and environment designs often made the leap from paper to computer renderings. Concept artists used programs such as Photoshop to produce their computer images (middle/left figure by concept sculptor Michael Murnane).

"Ninety-nine percent of that stuff was false," Gurland noted. "It made me giggle to read reports that I was someplace I'd never been, talking to people I'd never met. I started to think I had an evil twin out there somewhere!" One news item reported that Gurland was seen in Sydney, standing by a Fox Studios watercooler, discussing the casting. "They got the story so wrong, they didn't even have my *name* right. They said that 'casting director Lynne Hale was standing by a watercooler with a photo of Gabriel Byrne in her hand'—and Lynne Hale is the director of publicity for Lucasfilm! The person reporting this said that they had approached me/Lynne and said, 'Are you thinking of Gabriel Byrne for something?' Supposedly, I took the photo to my breast, said, 'None of your business,' and walked off in a huff. Of course, none of this ever happened! But suddenly rumors are flying that Gabriel Byrne is going to be in the movie."

Amid such intense media interest, Gurland initiated the Anakin search by viewing videotape or film submissions from hundreds of young actors. Physical characteristics were among the things Gurland was looking for—a blue-eyed, blond-haired actor who looked like a mature version of actor Jake Lloyd, who had portrayed Anakin as a young boy in Episode I. Age was another important consideration. The right actor had to be old enough to engage in a romance with twenty-four-year-old Padmé, as played by Natalie Portman, yet young enough to make believable his student–mentor relationship with Ewan McGregor's Obi-Wan Kenobi.

"I looked at people who were very appropriate, agewise, to people who were on the fringes, agewise," Gurland said. "From that wide base, I narrowed the choices down, making the determination that this one was a bit too old, or the look on that one wasn't right, or this one didn't have the necessary acting ability. There were many things to consider: the actor had to be

right physically, and he had to be the right age, but he also had to have an innate sensibility about him. He had to have a bit of an edge, yet be vulnerable. The role was really a person teetering on a fence—he is *this*, but you know just by looking at him that he could turn into *that*. Most actors have one or two characteristics that come to the forefront, but we had to find someone who could play all these different aspects of a personality."

Out of fifteen hundred submissions, Gurland selected four hundred actors with whom to meet in person, chatting informally with each for twenty minutes or so. "At those meetings," Gurland said, "I tried to gauge what the actor was like as a person. If I thought someone was a serious contender, I videotaped a next meeting. I ended up taping about one hundred actors, then chose thirty who fit all the requirements, and then gave those tapes to George and Rick."

From those thirty, Lucas selected the actors he thought had the most potential, all of whom he subsequently videotaped as they read scenes from the movie. Lucas then narrowed the field again. Finally, during the first week in May 2000—just seven weeks before filming—five Anakin finalists were given a screen test. "I brought that small group in to do a scene with Natalie, and shot it, just as we would the

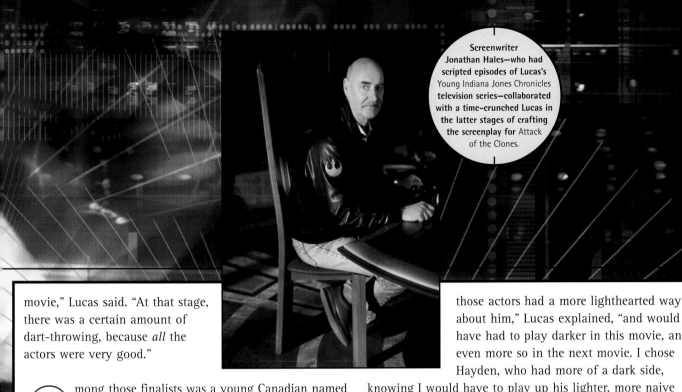

movie," Lucas said. "At that stage, there was a certain amount of dart-throwing, because *all* the actors were very good."

A mong those finalists was a young Canadian named Hayden Christensen, a virtual unknown who had done small supporting roles in films such as *The Virgin Suicides* and *In the Mouth of Madness* and, on television, had appeared in several movies of the week, as well as in the Fox Family Channel series *Higher Ground*. Though the ultimate decision would rest with Lucas, Gurland had been privately rooting for Christensen from the moment she had first met him. "I had a very strong sense about Hayden right off," Gurland admitted. "He was incredibly charismatic and nice—but there was something more than that. He had this easygoing, vulnerable side, but you could also see him developing into something dangerous."

Gurland's belief in Christensen's potential only magnified after the screen test. "When I saw him on camera," Gurland said, "he just popped! You could almost feel the electricity coming off the screen. So I was very excited, and I thought he was the right choice."

Lucas, too, had a strong initial reaction to Christensen, and chose him as one of the two final actors in contention for the role. "One of

those actors had a more lighthearted way about him," Lucas explained, "and would have had to play darker in this movie, and even more so in the next movie. I chose Hayden, who had more of a dark side, knowing I would have to play up his lighter, more naive side at the beginning of this movie, then gradually let his darker side come out."

To prepare for his life-changing role as Anakin Skywalker, Christensen carefully studied the four existing *Star Wars* films. "I engulfed myself in *Star Wars*," Christensen recalled. "It was nice because there was so much information—but it was also hard because Anakin Skywalker wasn't just *my* character. Other people had played him, and as much as I might have liked to make the character my own, I really couldn't. So I took note of who else had played the part, their mannerisms, and what they had brought to the role."

Christensen joined the ranks of Episode I veterans Natalie Portman, Ewan McGregor, and Samuel L. Jackson, whose Mace Windu character would play a more prominent role in the new film than in the last. New actors coming into the *Star Wars*

Padmé Amidala, a Queen in Episode I (below), serves as a Senator from Naboo in Attack of the Clones. Released from the pomp and formality of portraying a Queen, Portman was able to explore a broader emotional range for the new film.

fold for Episode II included Jimmy Smits, who would play Senator Bail Organa, and the legendary Christopher Lee as Count Dooku, an ex-Jedi who has turned to the dark side. To cast many of the film's secondary roles, Robin Gurland, once settled in Australia, attended the Sydney Film Festival and local theater productions to familiarize herself with Sydney's talent pool.

Like Gurland, Gavin Bocquet had been on the show for nearly a year by the time the June 2000 shoot date rolled around. In addition to accompanying McCallum on location scouts, Bocquet had prepared for the shoot by checking out Fox Studios in Sydney with supervising art director Peter Russell. "We made two trips to Sydney in July and August 1999," Bocquet recalled. "We needed to find out what we could achieve down there with local labor and facilities, and what we'd have to bring in."

Though Australia had developed a vital film industry, it had not traditionally been the home of large-scale productions at the level of *Star Wars*, so McCallum suspected Sydney might be limited in its number of experienced construction and art department personnel. Some of those crew members, he surmised, would have to be brought in from the United States and Great Britain—not a simple matter given

Australia's restrictive union regulations. McCallum found himself having to do some spirited negotiating.

"Rick's argument was that he couldn't take the film to Australia unless he was allowed to take this group of outside technicians in," Bocquet said. "It was a continuity issue: there were various sets that were going to be repeats from the last film, and it would be hard to have a completely new group of people building those sets. There was logic in taking people who had worked on the first film, people who *knew* Naboo and Tatooine and Coruscant. Rick negotiated all of that before he ever agreed to take this movie to Sydney."

One of the conditions of McCallum's arrangement with the unions was that the production would train a number of Australian workers on Episode II, preparing them to work on Episode III, which would also be filmed at Fox-Sydney. "That way," McCallum said, "we wouldn't need to bring in as many outside people for the next film. So we set up a training program for rigging and plaster work and wardrobe management, which benefited them as well as us."

Assured that some Episode I art department veterans would be allowed to work on the film, and having thoroughly explored the facilities at Fox, Bocquet began designing specific sets. Those new to Episode II were first built in

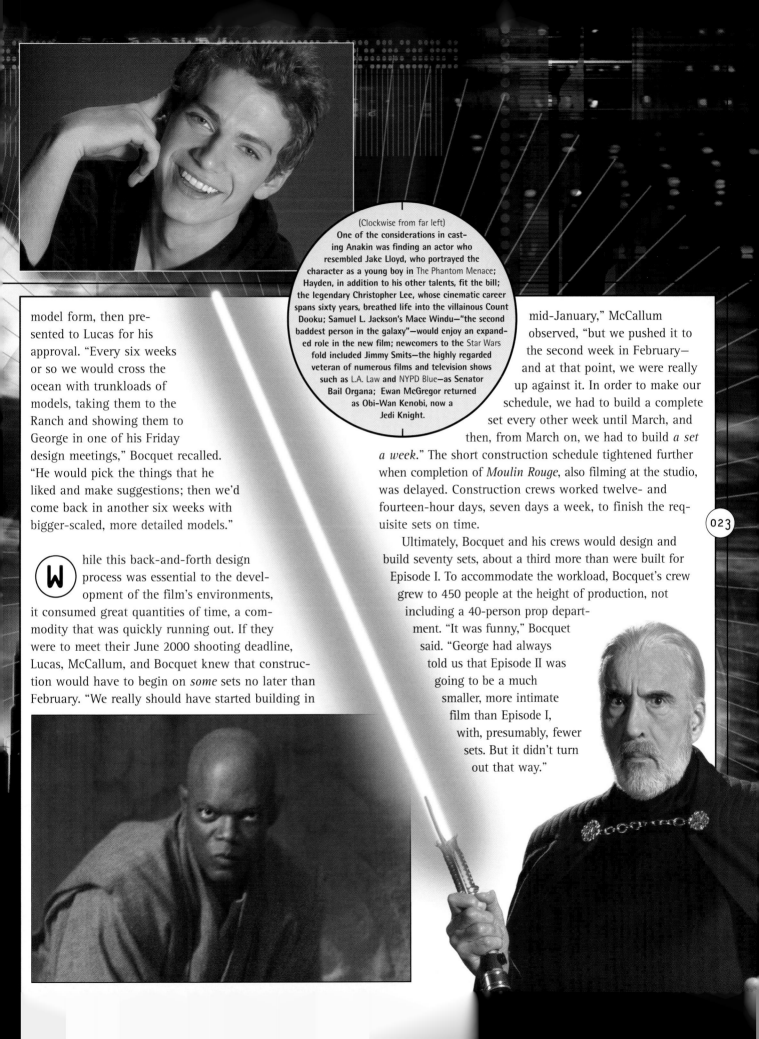

model form, then presented to Lucas for his approval. "Every six weeks or so we would cross the ocean with trunkloads of models, taking them to the Ranch and showing them to George in one of his Friday design meetings," Bocquet recalled. "He would pick the things that he liked and make suggestions; then we'd come back in another six weeks with bigger-scaled, more detailed models."

W hile this back-and-forth design process was essential to the development of the film's environments, it consumed great quantities of time, a commodity that was quickly running out. If they were to meet their June 2000 shooting deadline, Lucas, McCallum, and Bocquet knew that construction would have to begin on *some* sets no later than February. "We really should have started building in mid-January," McCallum observed, "but we pushed it to the second week in February— and at that point, we were really up against it. In order to make our schedule, we had to build a complete set every other week until March, and then, from March on, we had to build *a set a week*." The short construction schedule tightened further when completion of *Moulin Rouge*, also filming at the studio, was delayed. Construction crews worked twelve- and fourteen-hour days, seven days a week, to finish the requisite sets on time.

Ultimately, Bocquet and his crews would design and build seventy sets, about a third more than were built for Episode I. To accommodate the workload, Bocquet's crew grew to 450 people at the height of production, not including a 40-person prop department. "It was funny," Bocquet said. "George had always told us that Episode II was going to be a much smaller, more intimate film than Episode I, with, presumably, fewer sets. But it didn't turn out that way."

023

At Fox, six soundstages, ranging from medium-sized to cavernous, were available to the production, along with smaller shed-type buildings, bringing the total number of "stages" to nine. "We were trying to fit all the sets into every square inch of the studio," McCallum said, "which was about half the size of Leavesden, where we shot the last film. We took over the entire studio, and still it was a tight fit."

Scheduling made it even tighter. On Episode I, the production schedule had dictated that the main unit shoot first at Leavesden, move on to locations, then return for more studio filming, a plan that afforded plenty of time for construction crews to strike one group of sets and put up another. This time, once production moved into the studio, it would stay there until the main unit left for location work at the end of the schedule, which meant that all of the stage sets would have to be ready for filming sometime within the nine-week shooting period at Fox.

As Bocquet constructed sets in Sydney, costume designer Trisha Biggar designed and built costumes from her head-quarters in London. Biggar had actually started on the film just before November 1999, meeting with Lucas and the concept designers at Skywalker Ranch to determine the new film's costume requirements.

"We were going to be seeing many of the same charac-ters, and we were going back to some of the same planets," Biggar said, "so, as a start, I sifted through the things we had in storage from Episode I. Some things we wanted to use again; others we wanted to modify to denote the passage of time." Following her initial visit to the Ranch, Biggar traveled to Sydney to meet potential crew members and inspect the facilities, then returned to London.

One of Biggar's tasks at this stage was translating highly stylized sketches rendered by concept artists Dermot Power and Iain McCaig into workable, real-world designs. "We had to translate the concepts into something we could actually build and someone could actually wear," Biggar noted, "while still keeping the look George had approved in the sketch." Once concepts were refined, Biggar and a crew of fifteen set up a workshop in London and began producing "toiles"—basic shapes made out of calico, or other inexpen-sive materials—for gowns that would be worn by Natalie Portman as Padmé. When those were completed, Biggar and costume props supervisor Ivo Coveney traveled to Boston—where Portman was completing her first year at Harvard—to fit both the toiles and cardboard headdress mock-ups.

"Natalie was in the middle of her exams, and she was exhausted," Coveney recalled. "At one point, she fell asleep right in the middle of the fitting. Her head just rocked for-ward, and she was out!" After the fitting, Coveney returned

to London to construct the headdresses, which were slightly less elaborate for this film than for the last, due to Padmé's transition from Queen to Senator.

Portman's sixteen costumes numbered six more than what she had worn for Episode I, but overall the new movie's costume count equaled the one thousand built for that first film. "The number was about the same," Biggar said, "but they were of a different type. We didn't have masses of military costumes like we had for the last film. This time, we made more street costumes for ordinary townspeople in Coruscant or Naboo—more regular-people clothes, as opposed to elaborate ceremonial clothing."

Biggar and her crew—which, at the peak of production, numbered more than one hundred people, with up to sixty "cutters" alone required—had only six months in which to build those thousand-plus costumes. In her London workshop, and later in Sydney, Biggar oversaw the making of custom patterns. She also traveled extensively, in search of special materials that would give the costumes an appropriately exotic, *Star Wars* look. The chosen fabrics came from more than a dozen countries, including Japan, India, China, and Indonesia. When Biggar couldn't find a specific fabric or material, she would have it custom-made.

T he last of the major departments to gear up for the film was the visual effects team at Industrial Light & Magic, which would produce most of its shots in the eighteen

025

Like its predecessors, *Attack of the Clones* was populated with aliens portrayed by performers in foam latex masks. The production pulled from its stock of masks and costumes from the previous films—even some featured in the cantina scene in *Star Wars: A New Hope*—to create the new cast of background alien characters.

months following principal photography. As it had been for *The Phantom Menace*, the slate of visual effects for Episode II—which would ultimately number more than two thousand—was divided among several supervisors: John Knoll and Pablo Helman primarily oversaw those sequences featured in the first two-thirds of the film, with Knoll concentrating on a climatic arena battle while Ben Snow and Dennis Muren supervised much of the film's clone war sequence. Preliminary work began with Knoll six months before the start of filming.

"At first we just had meetings here and there," Knoll recalled, "and then we started full time in May, figuring out what we needed for the shoot, such as lighting reference maquettes for the computer-generated characters, which had been very useful on Episode I. We'd had a full-sized Jar Jar head and a full-sized Watto maquette on stage that we could put under the lights, providing us important reference when it came time to put our CG characters into the scene. They were useful for David Tattersall, the director of photography, as well, because he was able to light more than just an empty set. And it was helpful as a communication tool for the actors. We could tell them, 'This is who you are talking to in the scene.'"

Knoll and a small ILM contingent arrived in Sydney in the middle of June, approximately two weeks before the start of shooting, to answer visual-effects-related questions from various department heads. Knoll collaborated most closely with Gavin Bocquet, because inherent in every scene was the question of how much should be built as a practical stage set and how much should be filled in with digital set extensions or miniatures in post-production.

All of the separate departments had come together by the time filming commenced in Sydney on June 26, 2000—coincidentally, three years to the day after the first day of shooting Episode I. For many, coming off a year of preparation and planning, of designing, writing, scouting, casting, negotiating, and hiring, the day felt like a culmination of sorts.

In truth, it was only the beginning.

june 26, 2000
fox studios, sydney

Cast and crew members have assembled for the first day of principal photography on *Star Wars:* Episode II *Attack of the Clones.* On the agenda is a scene in the Senate Hall, where Chancellor Palpatine and a contentious Senate prepare to vote on the controversial Military Creation Act.

In the finished film, the Senate chamber will be a vast, digitally extended space filled with floating pods and hundreds of computer-generated galactic representatives—but its physical representation on stage today is modest. There are only Palpatine's podium, mounted on a base to raise it several feet from the stage floor, and a similarly mounted pod. At the podium, actor Ian McDiarmid, as Palpatine, addresses an invisible assembly of Senators, whose lines of dialogue are read off-camera by the script supervisor. Bluescreen surrounds the stage, creating a matte area into which Industrial Light & Magic will insert its expansive digital set.

The mood is light on this first day. George Lucas, showing no signs of the pressure of mounting so large-scale a production, iquietly talks and jokes with the cast and crew, all of whom wear jackets to protect them from the early-morning chill. June 26 is winter in Australia.

It is "do or die" day for the new high-definition digital cameras, being used for the first time on a major feature film. They appear to be working well—although, between takes, technicians scramble to solve a problem with the cameras' power supply. "Don't worry," producer Rick McCallum assures the camera operators. "It's just the first day. We'll figure it out. This is 'Earn As You Learn Productions' for the first couple of weeks."

Outside the stage, Anthony Daniels suits up as C-3PO for the first time in thirteen years. Daniels sighs and says, "Ah, yes, I remember this well," as droid unit supervisor Don Bies attaches the metallic breastplate, arm, and leg sections of the suit. Once the head is secured, Bies flips a switch and the eyes light up. C-3PO is suddenly, unquestionably *there*.

Accompanied by Bies and his assistants, Daniels shuffles toward the stage for a significant reunion with George Lucas. Unable to see well through the mask, he is guided over cables and power cords and carefully led around lights and camera equipment.

"I'd forgotten how lonely it is in here," Daniels says, his voice muffled from within the metallic head.

The reactions from crew members as Daniels makes his slow and clumsy way through the stage belie his words. All of them smile broadly, and say, "Hello, Threepio," when they see him. One says, "I'd shake your hand, but mine are dirty." With characteristic prissiness, C-3PO steps back, aghast.

He finally arrives at George Lucas's side. "Hello, I'm See-Threepio," Daniels says in the droid's mannered voice, extending his hand. "And you are?"

"I am...astonished," Lucas says. "Astonished that you can still get into that suit. Wish I could do it," he adds, smiling ruefully and patting his stomach.

(Top) The production office of Fox Studios, Australia; (below) The first day of filming centered on a scene—cut from the final movie—in which Chancellor Palpatine announces the assassination of Senator Padmé Amidala to the assembly of galactic representatives. Ian McDiarmid, shown here in a later Senate scene, was shot on a lectern on a bluescreen stage; ILM added the entire senate chamber and its inhabitants as digital effects in post-production.

chapter
two

on coruscant

A long time ago in a galaxy far, far away....

I n the opening of *Attack of the Clones*, as that quintessentially *Star Wars* legend scrolls into infinity, a chrome-plated Naboo royal cruiser escorted by three yellow starfighters enters the frame and descends into the galactic capital of Coruscant. Moments after Senator Padmé Amidala and her entourage emerge from their ships, a violent explosion destroys the cruiser, throwing the entire party to the landing platform floor. Kneeling to attend to the wounded Senator, a female pilot removes her helmet—revealing Padmé's beautiful, familiar face. Captain Typho (Jay Laga'aia), Padmé's security officer, looks on as she cradles in her arms her dying decoy, Cordé (Veronica Segura).

Opening shots of the spacecraft and cityscape were computer-generated at ILM many months after the end of principal photography, but the live-action scene that follows was captured during the second week of filming, on one of several platform sets built by Gavin Bocquet's art department and construction crews. "We had two stages where we built floors with

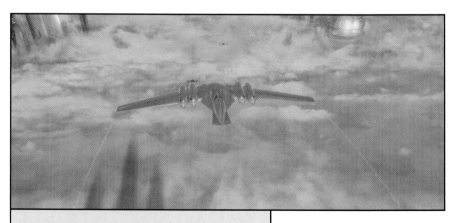

(Top and above) Attack of the Clones **opens with an approach to Coruscant—the Republic capital—by a Naboo royal cruiser and three Naboo starfighter escort craft. Industrial Light & Magic produced the visual effects shot, comprised of digital matte paintings and computer-generated starships.**

slightly different designs to represent different landing platforms," Bocquet explained. "The one on Coruscant was a three-leaf clover, with a ramp from the royal cruiser for Cordé and the others to climb down—but there was no ship there, of course. The rest of it was bluescreen." The platform measured one hundred feet by thirty feet and was made out of timber, then painted to give it a metallic appearance.

Though the set was minimal, it was extremely helpful to the visual effects team in that it created a grounding for

all the computer-generated images that would surround it. "At first," John Knoll recalled, "George was pushing pretty hard to shoot *everything* blue, including the platform floor, but I persuaded him to build the platform and the ladders descending from the ships. Character reflections and shadows are very difficult to fake with CG, so it was always preferable to have some set piece there, even if it was only a floor."

Though the explosion would be a digital effect, as well, onstage stunt performers created the illusion of interaction by reeling back on cue as if from the impact of the blast. Director of photography David Tattersall provided interactive lighting to suggest the explosion on set, setting up a pulsing, orange-filtered light to illuminate the performers. Stage debris and smoke, later augmented digitally, suggested the explosion's aftermath.

Filmed just days into the principal photography schedule, the landing platform scene was one of Natalie Portman's first upon arriving in Australia from Harvard. "Coming to Australia to work was a really good way to transition back into *Star Wars*," Portman said. "I had never been there, so it became part of this whole new *Star Wars* experience."

In the original script, the action moved to the Senate Hall, where galactic representatives debated the controversial Military Creation Act, legislation that would arm the Republic against a growing league of Separatists, led by ex-Jedi Count Dooku. The Senate setup on Stage 6, one of the studio's smaller stages, included one twenty-foot-diameter pod, raised three feet above the stage floor and surrounded on all sides with bluescreen so that CG pods filled with CG aliens could be added in post-production. The only other set piece was Palpatine's fifteen-foot-diameter podium, mounted on a stand covered in blue material so that it could be replaced with digital backgrounds to create the illusion that the podium was perched on a taller column.

One of the sets previously built for *The Phantom Menace*, the Senate was an easy assignment for the art and construction departments. Almost no construction would have been required, in fact—the original pod and podium had been stored in London—were it not for a cost breakdown that proved it would be more expensive to ship the items from London than to rebuild them in Australia. To make the most efficient use of the studio's limited stage space, the Senate set pieces were mounted on wheels so they could be rolled in and out, as needed, or repositioned quickly to accommodate different camera angles.

Beyond the live-action pod and podium, the entire Senate was a digital set created by ILM. Whenever possible, Lucas favored inserting digital sets into bluescreen areas

The production crew waits between setups of the platform scene on stage in Sydney. A newly completed studio drew the production to Australia, making Attack of the Clones the first Star Wars feature not based in England. (Below, left and center) Moments after landing, the royal cruiser explodes due to an assassination attempt on Padmé. On-set pyrotechnics and debris provided the immediate aftermath of a computer-generated ship explosion. (Below right) Padmé's decoy, Cordé, is fatally wounded in the blast.

(Clockwise from top left) McCallum readies the clapboard on June 26, 2000, the first day of principal photography at Fox Studios. Ian McDiarmid as Supreme Chancellor Palpatine, David Bowers as Mas Amedda, and Sandi Findlay as Sly Moore are first filmed against a bluescreen. ILM completes the shot, adding background elements as needed.

over building full stage sets. Not only did the approach save construction time and money, but it also afforded the director more flexibility in restaging shots after the fact. "The way most films are organized," Rick McCallum noted, "you see a three-second wide establishing shot, which tells the audience where they are. Usually, a great deal of time and effort go into those three seconds. However, if you can create that shot through a digital painting, it is much easier. So we shot with a lot of bluescreen, building real sets only to a certain height, which was slightly above our tallest actor in a scene. Most directors build everything, just to protect themselves. But George only builds what he needs."

Ahmed Best (left), the voice of Jar Jar Binks, Christensen (center), and McDiarmid (right) enjoy an impromptu "meet and greet" on the set.

Lighting these predominantly blue environments wasn't particularly difficult for David Tattersall, who was well versed in the technique, nor was it particularly enjoyable. "Bluescreen is a necessary, essential part of shooting *Star Wars*," Tattersall conceded, "but it isn't my favorite part. George is the only one who seems to like it. For me, it is just a necessary chore. It's much more fun to light a full environment. There's no artistry in lighting bluescreen; it is just a technical process." Concept paintings and sketches from the Ranch art department clued Tattersall, the actors, and other technicians as to what the completed sets would look like once the digital extensions were added. "Those helped me because they gave me some idea as to where the light would be coming from in a scene."

ILM had already built a 3D Senate Hall for Episode I, and that CG model was reemployed for Episode II. Visual effects supervisor Pablo Helman went through the backgrounds from Episode I's Senate scenes and pulled out half a dozen that could be used in conjunction with new foreground CG models. The library of Senate characters created for Episode I was also reused, augmented with new CG characters.

First on the schedule, the Senate Hall scene consumed days one and two of filming, an icebreaking period during which veteran members of the Episode I crew reunited and new crew members were introduced to the *Star Wars* family. "I remember being somewhat nervous that first day," admitted first assistant director James McTeigue, a member of the new Australian crew. "I thought everybody else was going to know exactly what they were doing, while I and the rest of the Australian crew were flailing about. But it

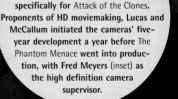

035

Director of photography David Tattersall behind one of the six prototype high-definition digital cameras built by Sony Engineering and Panavision specifically for Attack of the Clones. Proponents of HD moviemaking, Lucas and McCallum initiated the cameras' five-year development a year before The Phantom Menace went into production, with Fred Meyers (inset) as the high definition camera supervisor.

worked out fine. We'd prepped everything with George the week before we started, so everybody knew what to do. That got us off to a good start."

Day one on the Senate set featured Ian McDiarmid as Supreme Chancellor Palpatine at the podium, along with his majordomo, Mas Amedda (David Bowers in a latex mask). Despite his long association with the *Star Wars* saga—having portrayed the Emperor in *Return of the Jedi* and a younger Senator Palpatine in *The Phantom Menace*—McDiarmid, too, approached that first day with some trepidation.

"The script had just arrived at the last minute," McDiarmid explained. "I had a few long speeches in the Senate scene, but I'd only had three days to learn all those lines. I was in midair on this pod, there was a camera pointing right at me, and I was addressing crosses and markers rather than real actors. It was a new crew and there were new actors entering the *Star Wars* universe for the first time. All of those things were flying through my mind, and it was quite scary. However, I've learned that you can *use* that kind of fear if you can control it. The first few days were about taking charge of that fear."

Perhaps no nerves on the set were as frayed as those of the camera operators, because that first day of filming was the ultimate test of the new high-definition digital cameras Lucasfilm had developed in collaboration with

Sony and Panavision. At the time Episode I was released, Lucasfilm had issued a bold statement promising that Episode II would be shot entirely on high-definition (HD) videotape rather than on film—a first in a movie of this size. One of the primary reasons Lucas and McCallum wanted to go all digital was that in order to integrate the ubiquitous digital effects, film has to be transferred to a digitized format—a slow and expensive process. Digitizing the film for *The Phantom Menace* had cost $2.5 million; and then, once all the digital effects had been added, the movie had required scanning back out to film.

The HD cameras, which would run digital videotape that could be read and directly uploaded into the computer, would result in a movie that was *already* in a digital format, saving the step of digitizing the film. In the future, as more movie theaters invest in the appropriate digital projection systems, the step of scanning back out to film will also be eliminated. Movies will be all digital all the time, saving money and affording filmmakers maximum flexibility in constructing their images.

The development of the digital cameras had been a five-year project, initiated by Rick McCallum, with high definition supervisor Fred Meyers, working out of ILM, acting as technical point person between Lucasfilm and Sony.

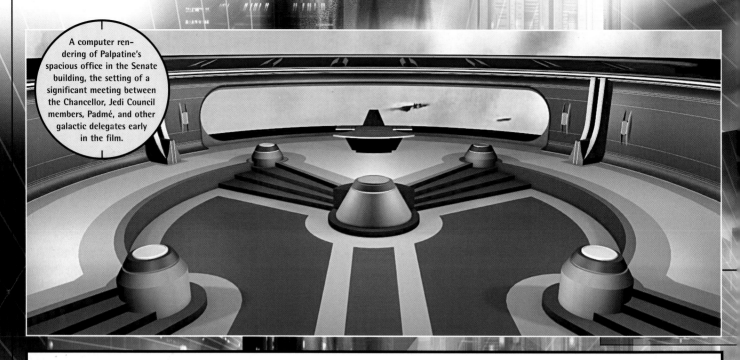

"With Sony," Meyers said, "we explored how HD cameras might be used as film camera replacements. The problem was to adapt them so that they would be suitable for a film application, rather than a video application." The focus was on the development of lenses that would be appropriate to a film shoot, as well as on frame rate and quality issues. "Currently, all film productions run cameras at twenty-four frames per second, whereas the HD cameras used by broadcasters run at twenty-five or thirty frames per second. We had to resolve those incompatibility issues."

David Tattersall, too, had been in on the development of the cameras throughout the five-year period. Still, it wasn't until January 2000—six months before the start of principal photography on *Attack of the Clones*—that

Padmé initially resists Palpatine's offer of Jedi protection. Computer-generated characters in the office scene—such as Jar Jar and Yoda—were added to live-action plates by ILM in postproduction.

Tattersall saw technological advancements that would make feasible the shooting of the movie on high-def. "At that time," Tattersall recalled, "there were two big improvements made. The first was Sony's development of the twenty-four-P system. *P* stands for 'progressive scan,'

which means that the video camera is recording at twenty-four frames per second, the same rate as a film camera and projector. That meant the high-def could be transferred to film, frame to frame, so there wouldn't be problems with thirty-cycle or sixty-cycle video speeds. The other big development was Panavision's invention of two new zoom lenses, designed specifically for a video chip, which were far ahead of anything else on the market. Those two things, in combination, made it possible to do this."

Even with those technological leaps, however, there was some controversy within the film community regarding Lucas's use of high-def over film for the new movie—a controversy that greatly puzzled the director. "People asked, 'Why are you doing this?'" Lucas recalled. "But the real question was, 'Why not?' It was vastly superior in every way, and it was cheaper. You'd have to be nuts *not* to shoot this way. As far as I was concerned, we should have been shooting digital cinema twenty years ago."

Lucas's faith in the technology was validated once the new cameras rolled on *Attack of the Clones*. In addition to their other advantages, the HD cameras—unlike film cameras, which require frequent reloading—could run all day without interruption. "At the start of every day they had to do focus checks and color balance checks," James McTeigue noted, "which took up a bit of time; but we more than made up that time throughout the day because we never had to load film. Once we got started with the digital camera, it was smooth running. From a technical point of view, the digital cameras had very few problems. They were fantastic!"

action situated in storms, at night, or in shadowy corridors.

As he oversees the contentious assembly from his podium, Chancellor Palpatine delivers a disturbing message (in a scene that was cut from the film): Senator Padmé Amidala has been assassinated. A bereaved hush falls over the chamber, interrupted by the arrival of Padmé

There was definitely a learning curve in the use of the digital cameras, though. In fact, the first time they were tested for the production was for a dinner scene between Anakin and Padmé. Although the actual filming of the scene was eventually postponed until later in the schedule, the set was dressed with stand-ins in costumes as a means of testing the cameras. Part of the learning curve was discerning how to adjust lighting for the digital video format, because it was less forgiving than film when it came to hard contrasts. To accommodate the format, David Tattersall took care to soften the lighting as much as possible, using silks, diffusion screens, and large bounce reflectors, while still adhering to the lighting style of previous *Star Wars* episodes.

"George always talked about there being a unified look to all the films," Tattersall said, "so I was aware of not going too far away from that. There are some trendy looks in movies these days, but George's photographic preferences are a bit more conservative. He has a certain look he has established, and he wants to stay with that." Episode II *would* distinguish itself from the other *Star Wars* films in that it was darker than its predecessors, with more of its

herself, very much alive and very much against the proposed legislation on the floor.

Padmé's new position as Senator, rather than Queen, was one of the more important points in the Lucas-Hales script. "I wanted to emphasize the point that the Republic was a democracy," Lucas explained. "I thought I'd made it clear in *The Phantom Menace* that Padmé was an elected official, but that point seemed to go right by everybody, probably because I used the word *Queen*, which suggested an inherited position of power. However, I had intended it as a designation of a ruler, like *president*. I only used the *princess/queen/knight* terminology because I was harking back to King Arthur and other romantic periods.

"This time, I wanted to reestablish the fact that Padmé had been *elected* as Queen, served her two terms in office, and then stepped down. It's the opposite of what Palpatine does. His term has run out in the intervening ten years, but he has been 'reluctantly' convinced to stay in office; as we go on, he'll be 'reluctantly' convinced to stay in office even longer. I wanted Padmé's character to be the example of what leaders *should* do, which is serve their term, then leave. The idea on Naboo is that you do your service when

(Left) Costume designer Trisha Biggar among many works in progress. (Right) Lucas looks on as Trisha attends to Smits.

you're very young—twelve to twenty-two—then you retire, have a family, and live the rest of your life. Padmé is an exception because she's now twenty-four. She did her service, but then she became a Senator because the new Queen asked her to."

For her part, Natalie Portman was happy to see Padmé's transformation from Queen to Senator, because it freed her from the restrictive and formal costumes and makeup she had been required to wear for the first film. Her new role also afforded more of an emotional range. "I was *very* excited that she wasn't going to be a Queen anymore," Portman said, "because it allowed the character to be more like a real person, as opposed to this regal facade of a person."

A less formal Padmé gave Trisha Biggar and her crew an opportunity to create a number of beautiful new costumes for Portman, including a Senatorial gown that Lucas first envisioned as softer and less ceremonial than anything she had worn as Queen. When Lucas saw the finished costume, however, he determined that the gown was a bit *too* soft and feminine for the strong Padmé.

"George decided to formalize her a bit more," Biggar explained, "and so this dress became quite stiff, as if it were corseted. We used royal colors for it, blue velvet

038

and gold, which looked very good on Natalie, connoted her royal past, and were rich, but without the aggressiveness of the reds she wore in the first film."

With the surprise arrival of Padmé in the Senate Hall, Palpatine adjourns the assembly and retires to his office, where he meets with Jedi Masters Yoda, Mace Windu, Plo Koon, and Ki-Adi-Mundi, as well as with Padmé and other galactic representatives, some portrayed by actors in masks or extensive makeup. Alien performers, who would spend up to nine hours in the makeup chairs, arrived at two o'clock that morning and shot all day long.

The scene in Palpatine's office was filmed on a large, circular set representing just one corner of the Chancellor's official domain. "It was a giant office," Gavin Bocquet noted. "After all, Palpatine is the head of the galaxy, so you can justify a really large office. To start, we took a concept sketch that George had signed off on and turned it into three or four alternatives in three-dimensional model form. He chose one of those, and then we made a bigger, more detailed model. The office design followed the modern art deco lines we'd established for all the Coruscant architecture."

Because the concept sketches were typically rendered in black ink, colors for Palpatine's office were determined in the model phase, with Bocquet using fabrics and paint samples to create color palettes from which Lucas could choose. Through color, Bocquet and Lucas strove to make a subtle connection between the Chancellor and the Emperor he would

Creatures supervisor Jason Baird applies finishing touches to a prosthetic makeup for Senator Passel Argente. Baird refurbished existing masks and prosthetic makeups in addition to building new characters as needed.

ultimately become. "We went back and forth with George as to whether the office should have the same bloodred color that you see in Palpatine's apartment in *The Phantom Menace*," Bocquet recalled, "or whether it should have blacks and grays to suggest Palpatine's turning to the dark side. We finally suggested that we make the office half red and half monochromatic grays and blacks. Then, in Episode III, if we show Palpatine's room or office, we can lose the red and make it *all* black to indicate his complete turn to the dark side. It created a character arc through color."

Those subliminal connections were also established in the furnishings provided by set decorator Peter Walpole and his crew, who custom-built settees, tables, a desk, and a chair for the set. "We built the chair very much in the style you see in the Emperor's chair in Episode VI," Walpole said, "so there was a bit of foreshadowing there and some continuity with the later film." In the course of production, Walpole oversaw thirty-odd model makers and an equal number of prop builders. "By the time we added it all up, we probably had a team of sixty or seventy. We tend not to add it up, though—because if Rick McCallum hears that we've employed sixty or seventy guys, he's sure to say: 'What are you doing with that big a crew! You only need five people!'"

The scene in Palpatine's office marked Yoda's first appearance in the film. Though Frank Oz would return to create Yoda's vocal performance, for the first time in *Star Wars* history, the character would be realized entirely

On the set in Sydney, Australia (from right to left): **Lucas, art director Jonathan Lee; set decorator Peter Walpole, and Gavin Bocquet.**

through computer animation rather than puppetry, a step Lucas had wanted to take for some time. He had, in fact, explored the possibility for *The Phantom Menace*, ultimately deciding that CG technology had not yet developed sufficiently. "There was one far-distance digital Yoda shot in the last movie," Lucas commented, "but we weren't in a place where we could do it in close-ups and make him look absolutely real. ILM probably *could* have done it, but I didn't want to lay that on them at the time. They were already working at one hundred percent to get the movie done, so I backed off that for *The Phantom Menace*.

"But on this one, I wanted to pursue the idea. So early on, when I first started writing the screenplay, I talked to John Knoll and Rob Coleman, the animation director, and asked, 'Do you think we can make it happen this time?' And they said: 'Yes, we can do it. We've made some advances.' And I said, 'Okay, then I'm going to treat Yoda in the script as if he were digital.' It allowed me to write him in a very different way. He could walk around, he could fight with a lightsaber. Before, I could only write scenes of Yoda sitting down, but a digital Yoda meant that I could treat him differently."

Tasked with overseeing all the computer animation for the film, Rob Coleman was elated by Lucas's decision. "One of the reasons I wanted to be involved in Episode II was to take on the challenge of creating Yoda digitally," Coleman admitted. "He is one of the most important in the pantheon

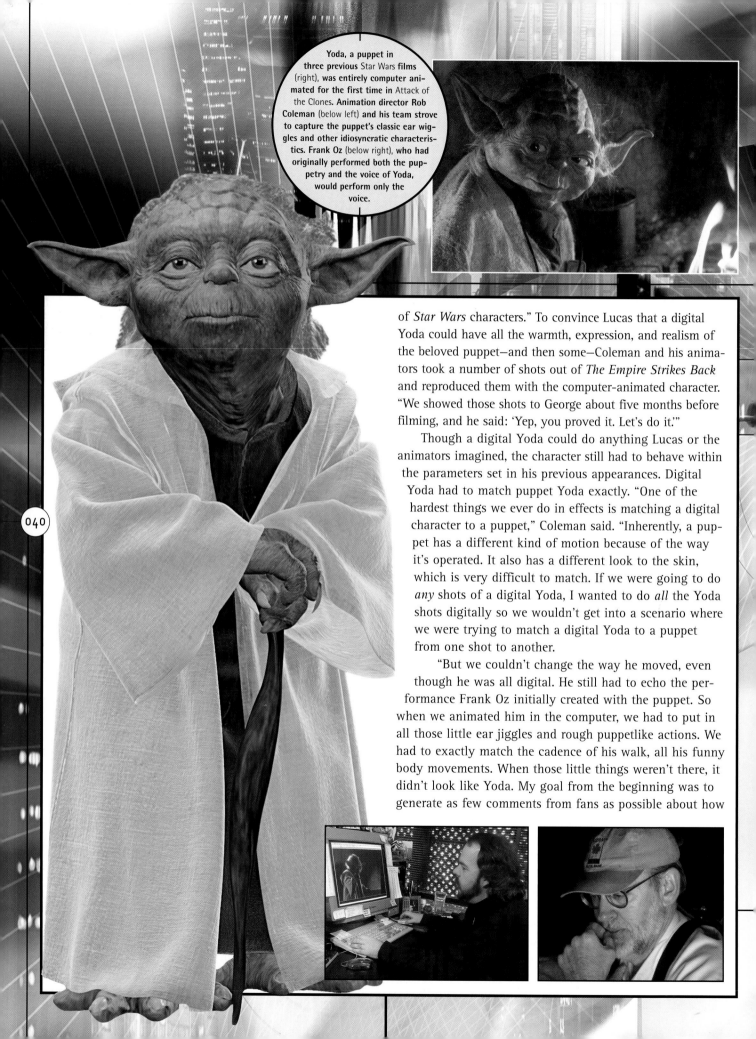

Yoda, a puppet in three previous Star Wars films (right), was entirely computer animated for the first time in Attack of the Clones. Animation director Rob Coleman (below left) and his team strove to capture the puppet's classic ear wiggles and other idiosyncratic characteristics. Frank Oz (below right), who had originally performed both the puppetry and the voice of Yoda, would perform only the voice.

of *Star Wars* characters." To convince Lucas that a digital Yoda could have all the warmth, expression, and realism of the beloved puppet—and then some—Coleman and his animators took a number of shots out of *The Empire Strikes Back* and reproduced them with the computer-animated character. "We showed those shots to George about five months before filming, and he said: 'Yep, you proved it. Let's do it.'"

Though a digital Yoda could do anything Lucas or the animators imagined, the character still had to behave within the parameters set in his previous appearances. Digital Yoda had to match puppet Yoda exactly. "One of the hardest things we ever do in effects is matching a digital character to a puppet," Coleman said. "Inherently, a puppet has a different kind of motion because of the way it's operated. It also has a different look to the skin, which is very difficult to match. If we were going to do *any* shots of a digital Yoda, I wanted to do *all* the Yoda shots digitally so we wouldn't get into a scenario where we were trying to match a digital Yoda to a puppet from one shot to another.

"But we couldn't change the way he moved, even though he was all digital. He still had to echo the performance Frank Oz initially created with the puppet. So when we animated him in the computer, we had to put in all those little ear jiggles and rough puppetlike actions. We had to exactly match the cadence of his walk, all his funny body movements. When those little things weren't there, it didn't look like Yoda. My goal from the beginning was to generate as few comments from fans as possible about how

(Far left) Obi-Wan Kenobi and Anakin Skywalker report to Padmé at her official residence. Jar Jar's greeting was shot first with Ahmed Best to give Christensen and McGregor a sense of timing and interaction, then without Best so that the CG Jar Jar could be inserted into a "clean" plate (left).

Yoda isn't the same because he's digital rather than a puppet, and so a tremendous amount of love and attention went into the character."

To give the live actors something to work off in their dialogues with Yoda in Palpatine's office, Jar Jar Binks vocal performer Ahmed Best acted the character during rehearsals, doing his best impression of Frank Oz's Yoda voice. Best had to perform double duty, since Jar Jar was present in the scene, as well. "I did a lot of filling in for characters who weren't there and voices that hadn't yet been cast," Best explained. "Rather than have someone just read those lines from offscreen, George asked me to learn the lines and perform with the other actors so the scene would have the proper timings." When it came time to actually film the scene, Best performed Yoda's and Jar Jar's lines off-camera to allow the digital characters to be inserted into a clean plate.

In the original Lucas-Hales screenplay, the ten-years-older Jar Jar was to have gone through a transformation from bungling Gungan to dignified Senator, complete with refined manners and speech, dubbed "diplodialect"—although he would lapse back into his idiosyncratic demeanor and style of speech in moments of high excitement. During principal photography, Best performed his lines with a wonderfully upper-crust, Ronald Colman–esque delivery.

By the time Lucas assembled a first cut of the film, however, he had decided to nix Jar Jar's new personality. "It was a funny idea," Lucas explained, "but when I looked at the first cut, I realized that it needed more explanation to make it work, and I didn't want to devote that much screen time to it, especially since Jar Jar is a secondary character. Given a choice of fleshing out the idea or cutting it all together, I decided to cut it." The decision had little impact on the production, because Jar Jar's animation was still in its beginning stages and Best had yet to record his lines for the final sound mix.

In addition to reintroducing Jar Jar Binks and Yoda, the scene in Palpatine's office featured Mace Windu and Senator Bail Organa. Bail Organa is a significant name in the *Star Wars* lexicon, because he would ultimately raise Padmé and Anakin's daughter, Leia. Their scene together in Palpatine's office was not the first collaboration for Samuel L. Jackson and Jimmy Smits. "Jimmy and I did theater together years ago," Jackson recalled, "before anybody knew who either of us was. It was great to work with a friend who brought such a good vibe to the set."

Smits was pleased but surprised when his agent called to tell him that Lucas was interested in having him appear in the next *Star Wars* film. "Just to be a part of something that has this kind of tradition and lore was really exciting," Smits said. "So I met Robin Gurland, and we hit it off. Then I talked to George, and he said he was a fan of my work and that there was a role in this movie he wanted me to check out. He said, 'Would you come play with us for a while in Australia?' I said: 'You got it! You don't even have to tell me what it's about, I'll be there!'

"The interesting thing about the experience was that, even though I was a fan of the films, I found that there were a lot of people who were *true* aficionados, who knew everything down to the most minute detail. When I mentioned to some people that I was playing this character, they rattled off who Bail Organa is and who he is related to and the history of each of those people. I had to go to the *Star Wars Encyclopedia* to figure it all out."

In light of the assassination attempt against Padmé, the Chancellor decides that more protection is in order and suggests that Padmé's old friend Obi-Wan Kenobi be assigned to safeguard her. That evening, Obi-Wan and his now twenty-year-old apprentice, Anakin Skywalker, report for duty at Padmé's quarters. Early versions of the screenplay had introduced the pair in the hall just outside Padmé's apartment, with tensions between Master and Padawan already flaring. Another of the decisions made by Lucas, upon his viewing of the first cut, was that an additional

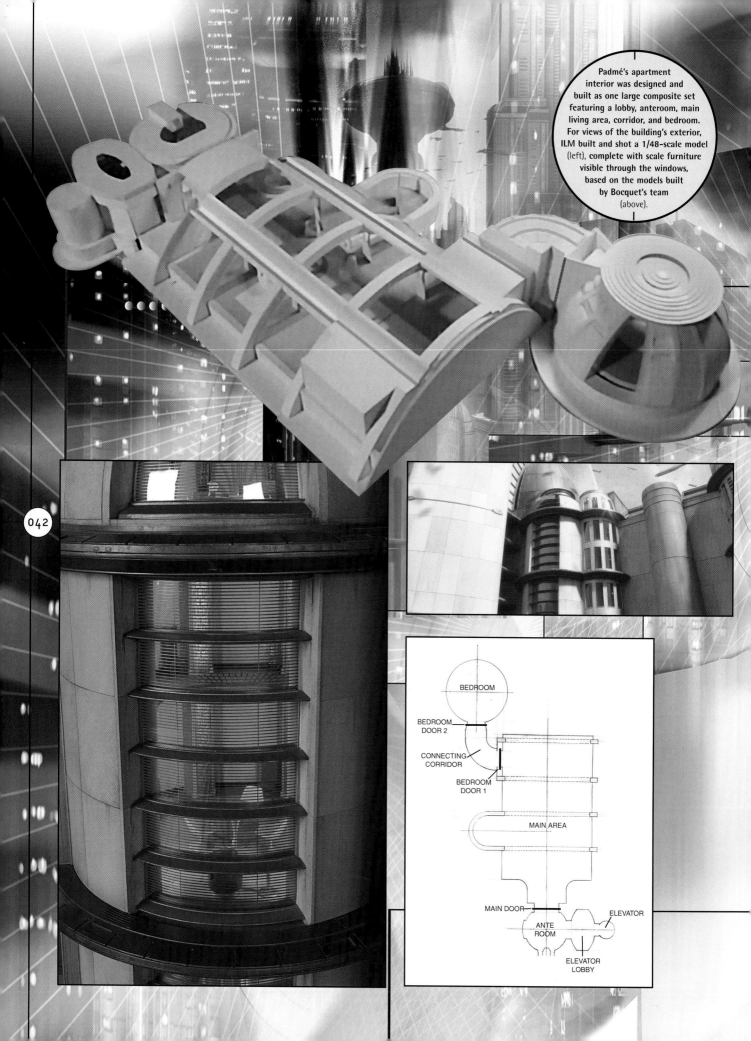

Padmé's apartment interior was designed and built as one large composite set featuring a lobby, anteroom, main living area, corridor, and bedroom. For views of the building's exterior, ILM built and shot a 1/48-scale model (left), complete with scale furniture visible through the windows, based on the models built by Bocquet's team (above).

BEDROOM

BEDROOM DOOR 2

CONNECTING CORRIDOR

BEDROOM DOOR 1

MAIN AREA

MAIN DOOR

ELEVATOR

ANTE ROOM

ELEVATOR LOBBY

B. PADME'S APT - MAIN COLOURWAYS   PAGE 1

SUGGESTED COLOURWAY FOR MAIN AREA AND BEDROOM

Primarily in the light and dark grey/blues. David Tattersall would prefer the walls and ceilings in the MAIN AREA to be these lighter tones, which will help him in the dusk scene.

PMS 644 C

PMS 643 C

PMS 430 C

PMS 540 C

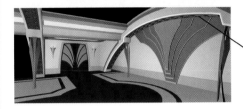

POLISHED BRONZE DETAIL

For the BEDROOM, we are suggesting these darker BLUE tones, to suggest a slightly more intimate area.

POLISHED WHITE-GOLD DETAIL

PMS 540 C

PMS 541 C

(Above left) **Gavin Bocquet's suggested color palette for the Padmé apartment set.**
(Above right) **Set models of the apartment interiors and exteriors.**

scene was needed in the elevator leading up to the Senate apartment, to more firmly establish the friendly, affectionate relationship between Obi-Wan and Anakin.

"In that first cut," Lucas explained, "the student–mentor relationship between Obi-Wan and Anakin was pretty rough right away, which got everything off to a bad start. Then, throughout the rest of the film, Obi-Wan is tough on Anakin, and Anakin is upset about how Obi-Wan treats him. After seeing the movie, I realized that we needed to soften their relationship a little bit, so the audience would see that they are actually friends. So I added this new scene in the elevator to establish that they actually *like* each other. All the way through the movie, I had to find a delicate balance between their affection for each other and the tension that is always there between them." The new scene was shot on a bluescreen stage in November 2001, during the second of three pickup shoots at Ealing Studios in London.

The action picks up as originally scripted once the duo is inside Padmé's apartment, a set designed to reflect an official environment. The vestibule, main living area, and bedroom were all built as one composite set on Stage 1, once a giant exhibition hall. "This stage was absolutely huge," Gavin Bocquet said, "bigger than anything we had at Leavesden for Episode I. It was about three hundred feet long and one hundred twenty feet wide. So we had the space to build this one enormous composite set for Padmé's apartment, which gave George the freedom to stage those scenes in a number of different ways."

Translated from concept sketches, the final penthouse set featured royal blue and gold walls, and floor-to-ceiling expanses of glass to accommodate Coruscant skyline vistas,

043

Senator Amidala greets Obi-Wan Kenobi and his Padawan, Anakin Skywalker, inside her official Senate apartment. The reunion is significant for Anakin, who has harbored strong feelings for the beautiful Padmé since boyhood.

which would be provided by ILM. "The daytime cityscapes in that scene were a very bold choice on George's part," Rick McCallum remarked. "We could have done beautiful night exteriors outside those windows, but George wanted to do a day sequence, which was much harder. In order for it to work, it had to look absolutely photoreal, and it had to have exactly the right light. I asked George, 'Are you sure you want to do this?' And he said, 'Yeah, let's go for it.'"

Padmé's apartment was a favorite for both Bocquet and set decorator Peter Walpole, because it provided an opportunity to create a more personal space than the spaceship interiors so often on the production design agenda. "It was a stunning piece of design," Walpole said, "like a fantastic, high-rise New York apartment. We found a company in Australia that made a style of furniture George liked. There was one settee, in particular, that George liked very much, and they made two of those settees for us, which dominated the center of the set. Overall, the style of furniture had a nineteen fifties or sixties feel to

it. To me, it was a bit like *The Jetsons'* furniture." Walpole decorated the set with unusual knickknacks, such as pieces of driftwood, wooden bowls, and dark licorice soap. "George liked what we put on the set, I think. He's a quiet gentleman and not a great enthuser—so if he *doesn't* say anything, that's how you know he likes what you've done."

The reunion with Padmé in her apartment is significant for Anakin, who for ten years has nurtured fond memories of the young Queen he befriended as a boy. Although frustrated by the intrusion of even more security, Padmé is warmed by the presence of her old friend Obi-Wan—and somewhat taken aback by little Annie's transformation to manhood.

"It starts out that her relationship with Anakin is one of mentor," Natalie Portman explained. "She's known him only as a little boy prior to this episode, so when they reencounter each other, she treats him like a little kid. George worked with me to make me seem older than Anakin, to make it believable that she would boss him around and look at him as a little boy—at least for the first half of the film, until it becomes more of a romance."

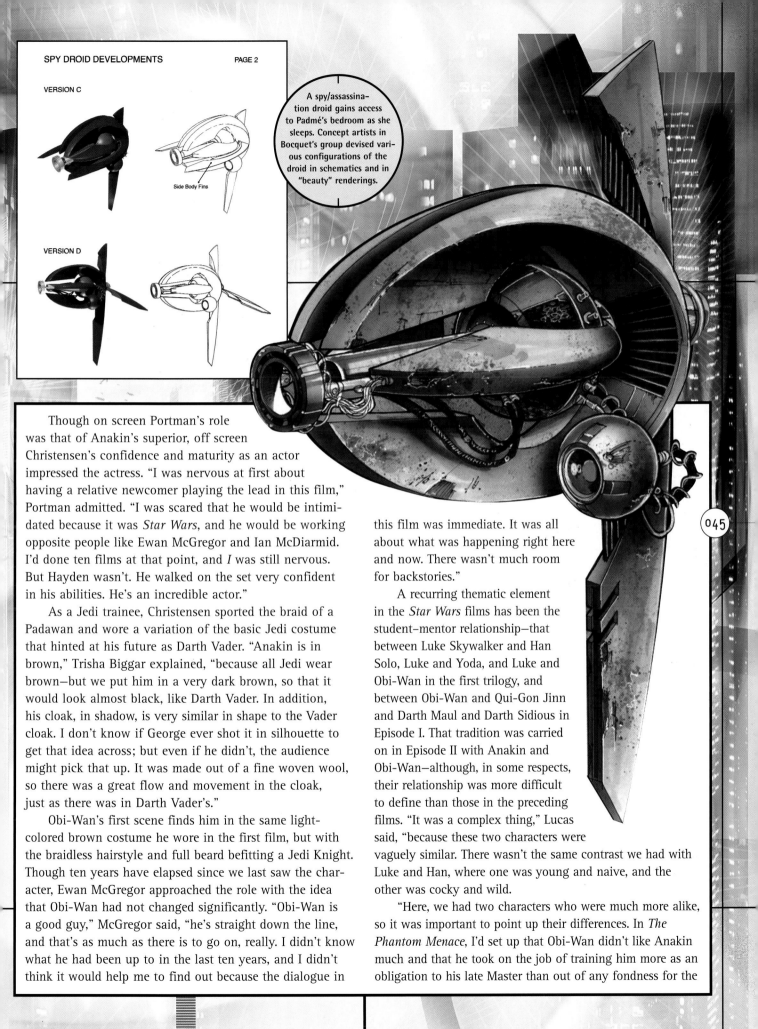

Side Body Fins

VERSION D

A spy/assassina-
tion droid gains access
to Padmé's bedroom as she
sleeps. Concept artists in
Bocquet's group devised various configurations of the
droid in schematics and in
"beauty" renderings.

045

Though on screen Portman's role was that of Anakin's superior, off screen Christensen's confidence and maturity as an actor impressed the actress. "I was nervous at first about having a relative newcomer playing the lead in this film," Portman admitted. "I was scared that he would be intimidated because it was *Star Wars*, and he would be working opposite people like Ewan McGregor and Ian McDiarmid. I'd done ten films at that point, and *I* was still nervous. But Hayden wasn't. He walked on the set very confident in his abilities. He's an incredible actor."

As a Jedi trainee, Christensen sported the braid of a Padawan and wore a variation of the basic Jedi costume that hinted at his future as Darth Vader. "Anakin is in brown," Trisha Biggar explained, "because all Jedi wear brown—but we put him in a very dark brown, so that it would look almost black, like Darth Vader. In addition, his cloak, in shadow, is very similar in shape to the Vader cloak. I don't know if George ever shot it in silhouette to get that idea across; but even if he didn't, the audience might pick that up. It was made out of a fine woven wool, so there was a great flow and movement in the cloak, just as there was in Darth Vader's."

Obi-Wan's first scene finds him in the same light-colored brown costume he wore in the first film, but with the braidless hairstyle and full beard befitting a Jedi Knight. Though ten years have elapsed since we last saw the character, Ewan McGregor approached the role with the idea that Obi-Wan had not changed significantly. "Obi-Wan is a good guy," McGregor said, "he's straight down the line, and that's as much as there is to go on, really. I didn't know what he had been up to in the last ten years, and I didn't think it would help me to find out because the dialogue in this film was immediate. It was all about what was happening right here and now. There wasn't much room for backstories."

A recurring thematic element in the *Star Wars* films has been the student–mentor relationship—that between Luke Skywalker and Han Solo, Luke and Yoda, and Luke and Obi-Wan in the first trilogy, and between Obi-Wan and Qui-Gon Jinn and Darth Maul and Darth Sidious in Episode I. That tradition was carried on in Episode II with Anakin and Obi-Wan—although, in some respects, their relationship was more difficult to define than those in the preceding films. "It was a complex thing," Lucas said, "because these two characters were vaguely similar. There wasn't the same contrast we had with Luke and Han, where one was young and naive, and the other was cocky and wild.

"Here, we had two characters who were much more alike, so it was important to point up their differences. In *The Phantom Menace*, I'd set up that Obi-Wan didn't like Anakin much and that he took on the job of training him more as an obligation to his late Master than out of any fondness for the

Bounty hunters Jango Fett and Zam Wesell meet to plot Padmé's assassination. The small ledge on which the actors performed was surrounded by digital matte paintings and 3D computer-generated sets.

boy. I had set up some friction between them. But at the same time, I wanted them to have a friendship."

"Anakin loves Obi-Wan because he is a father figure," Hayden Christensen added. "But at the same time, there's resistance because Anakin wants to break free, a theme in all of the *Star Wars* movies. So there is conflict and animosity between the characters when Obi-Wan won't let him make his own choices." Not surprisingly, given the ages of the actors, some of the more positive aspects of the Master–Padawan relationship made their way into Christensen's on-set relationship with McGregor. "I picked up some things from Ewan—the way he carried himself, certain Jedi mannerisms, such as the way the hands are held in the back. Ewan was a great guy and we got along well; and I think that dynamic was evident in the Obi-Wan–Anakin relationship. As an actor, I looked up to him, and that helped create a sense of Anakin looking up to Obi-Wan."

Following the reunion of Padmé, Obi-Wan, Anakin, and Jar Jar, the action cuts from Padmé's apartment to a skyscraper ledge and a meeting between bounty hunters Jango Fett (Temuera Morrison) and a veiled Zam Wesell (Leeanna Walsman), who plot to carry out the assassination of the Senator from Naboo. The scene, which was not in the original script, was shot at

Ealing Studios in March 2001. "I added that scene to show that our heroes were in peril," Lucas explained. "Before, people talked about them being in peril, but we never saw it. By cutting to this scene, I was able to create more of a sense of danger and tension."

From the outset, Jango had been conceived as a predecessor to the original trilogy's Boba Fett. The character of Zam, however, evolved many times over, from human male bounty hunter, to human female bounty hunter, to alien, to, finally, a changeling—known as a Clawdite—capable of

(Above) Leeanna Walsman—whom Robin Gurland discovered performing in a Sydney theatrical production—was cast as Zam Wesell in her human form. (Right) Concept sculptor Murnane sculpted a maquette of the character, the basis for the wardrobe department's final costume.

(Right) Natalie Portman and actress Rose Byrne (Dormé) share a laugh between takes of the bedroom scene in Padmé's apartment. (Below) Droid unit supervisor Don Bies and droid unit coordinator Zeynep Selcuk attend to one of the R2-D2 units employed during production.

taking any form. The notion of Zam as a changeling gelled after Lucas had returned from the shoot in Sydney, but the idea had been in the back of his head for a long time. "I'd thought of it early on," he said, "but I never pursued it. Then, once I saw the cut, I decided to put it in again. I thought Zam needed to be more exotic and interesting, and this was a way to do that."

The film would portray Zam in two forms: that of a grotesque alien, computer-generated by ILM, and, most often, that of a female person, portrayed by Walsman, a young Australian actress whom Robin Gurland had discovered performing in a play in Sydney. For her role as Zam, Walsman wore a tight-fitting costume clad with forty-five pieces of armor that were sculpted and fabricated by Ivo Coveney's costume prop department. "Because everything had to be movable on her," Coveney said, "each little part had to be sculpted separately and then fit together. The biggest problem with this costume—and this applied to many of Natalie's costumes, as well—was that the concept designers had drawn it and even sculpted a maquette of it on a totally unrealistic body shape that didn't correspond to a real person. The arms, legs, and torso were unnaturally long and thin. The figure looked like it was six feet tall, with more than half that length in the legs. So, inevitably, the shapes we came up with were somewhat different than the original designs."

Back inside the apartment, her Jedi protectors at the ready, Padmé retires for the night. The scene was shot in the bedroom of the composite apartment set, early in the principal photography schedule. "We had a lot of fun with Natalie doing that scene with Padmé in bed," Rick McCallum recalled. "When we'd first started working with Natalie, on Episode I, she'd been a girl of fifteen, under the care of her parents. This time, we were with a grown woman who was going to Harvard, *without* her parents. That day, for me, defined her as this new, adult person."

While Obi-Wan and Anakin discuss politics, R2-D2 watches over their sleeping charge. Droid unit supervisor Don Bies refurbished a number of existing R2-D2 units at

july 4, 2000
fox studios, sydney

There are no fireworks, picnics, or barbecues for the American members of the Attack of the Clones company on this Fourth of July—a cold and drizzly day marking the end of the shoot's second week.

On today's schedule are scenes staged inside Padmé's Coruscant apartment. The set is an austere, official residence, with powder-blue walls and floor-to-ceiling windows. To create appropriate contrast with the set's blue walls, greenscreen rather than bluescreen has been hung in the giant windows, so that ILM can eventually add a digital view of the Coruscant skyline.

The upcoming scene is a heated one between Padmé and Anakin as they prepare to leave Coruscant for the safety of Naboo. George Lucas goes over the action with his camera operators, telling them where he wants the cameras set and what kind of movement he would like to see. Stand-ins for Natalie Portman and Hayden Christensen position themselves on the set so that director of photography David Tattersall can make final lighting adjustments. First assistant director James McTeigue refers to the stand-ins as "Natalie" and "Hayden" as he moves them through their blocking.

The real Natalie and Hayden, in costume and makeup, arrive on the set and walk through the scene. As Portman rehearses her blocking, Lucas pulls Christensen to another part of the set to show him where Anakin will pick up an object and play with it in the air, courtesy of his telekinetic Force powers. Christensen will mime the action, and the floating object will be added as a digital effect in postproduction.

The actors and camera crew run a rehearsal of the scene. As the camera follows Christensen to the other side of the room, Portman—now out of frame—speaks her lines while crouching beside a camera so that her costar will be able to maintain eye contact with her. On Lucas's "Cut!" the makeup crew comes in to touch-up the actors' faces.

Minutes later, a first take of the scene is shot. Just prior to shooting a second take, Lucas instructs Christensen to tone down his mimed actions with the floating object this time through, to make them smaller and more subtle.

"Do not abuse your Jedi powers," Lucas jokes to the young actor; then, turning to Portman and jutting his thumb toward Christensen: "It's his first day with the Force—he's a little excited."

(Above) Anakin uses his Jedi powers to suspend an art object in the air. Christensen mimed the action on the set; then ILM added the digital object to the plate. (Below) ILM also inserted moving CG traffic and a digital matte-painted skyline into the set windows.

049

The droid at Padmé's bedroom window releases poisonous, insectlike "kouhuns." The creatures, droid, and window were all realized digitally by ILM.

ILM, modifying them to house a new and improved battery pack, and doing cosmetic touch-ups. The cosmetic upgrade was due to the British crew on Episode I having given the droid a slightly different paint job than that sported in the first three films. "We went back to the look that was in the first *Star Wars*," Bies explained, "matching the original blue, two-stage paint job. So Artoo-Detoo looks a bit different in Episode II than he did in Episode I."

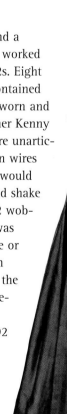

Once on set, Bies and a three-person crew worked with fifteen R2-D2s. Eight were radio-controlled, self-contained units; two were meant to be worn and articulated by R2-D2 performer Kenny Baker; and the remainder were unarticulated stunt models, towed on wires or puppeteered by Bies, who would grab the unit from behind and shake it to create the excited R2-D2 wobble. In postproduction, Bies was either positioned out of frame or painted out digitally. Between the improved mechanics and the ability to paint out an outside-the-unit puppeteer, Kenny Baker's role in bringing R2-D2 to life was reduced dramatically and, in the end, the veteran of all four previous *Star Wars* films was featured in only one shot.

The filming of the bedroom scene—and *any* scene featuring the

Biggar and crew designed an elegant gown for Senator Padmé.

diminutive R2-D2—made for a fun day on the set. "As soon as Artoo-Detoo comes on the set, everyone goes a bit silly," said Ewan McGregor, recalling his first few days of filming with the droid. R2-D2's appeal was brought home to the actor when his own then four-year-old daughter announced she was in love with him. "My daughter wants to marry him. She actually cried herself to sleep one night because she wasn't with Artoo. 'I love him, where is he?' She cried herself to sleep over a robot! It's funny—I don't personally want to marry Artoo-Detoo, but there is something about him that makes you feel great affection for him. I think it is a combination of his shape, his high-pitched voice. He's just incredibly appealing. In fact, I believe he is George's favorite actor."

With R2-D2 watching Padmé asleep in her bedroom and Anakin and Obi-Wan on alert in the main living quarters, all is quiet. Within moments, however, outside the window of Padmé's bedroom, an assassin droid cuts a hole through the glass. Inserting a tube through the hole, the assassin droid releases two poisonous, insectlike kouhuns. The foot-long, multilegged kouhuns, computer-modeled to resemble a cross between a centipede and a caterpillar, were among the challenging animation assignments for the team at ILM.

"Not only did they have all those legs," Rob Coleman said, "they had to go around and over objects. We created a path that they would move along, and then the animation software told the legs where to go along that path. That way, we didn't have to animate every single leg, which would have taken forever."

051

(Below) Visual effects supervisor John Knoll on the set with Portman. (Middle) Anakin slices the creatures in half as they near Padmé's face. (Bottom) The many appendages on the kouhuns required that ILM develop a computer-driven walk cycle, as hand-animating every leg would have been too time-consuming and labor-intensive.

Sensing a disturbance, Obi-Wan and Anakin burst into the room just as the kouhuns reach Padmé's face, and Anakin deftly cuts them in half with his lightsaber. Spotting the ASN-121 assassin droid outside the window, Obi-Wan crashes through the glass and grabs hold of the droid as it flies away. Production captured Obi-Wan's crash through the window both from the interior and the exterior of the set, with Ewan McGregor and a stunt double performing different pieces of the action.

All of the scenes in Padmé's apartment were completed in three days, the only time throughout production when Lucas tarried on a set for more than a single day. "And that was only because there were so *many* scenes there," McTeigue explained. "That's very unusual for filmmaking, and it surprised me. When we initially worked out the schedule, I was skeptical as to whether or not we could really move through the shoot at that pace. Everyone said, 'Don't worry, that's how George shoots.' My experience is that directors *don't* move that fast and *don't* do that many setups per day. However, George really did work that fast! We rocketed through, shooting an average of thirty-six setups a day, whereas fifteen setups per day are more typical. One day, he shot fifty-six setups! It was extraordinary. From an assistant director's point of view, it was fantastic to have a director who was that conscious of the schedule, and so willing to follow it."

chapter
three

on coruscant:
in the skies

Obi-Wan's jump from Padmé's bedroom window marks the beginning of the airspeeder chase, one of the film's most exciting and visually daring action sequences. Bluescreen elements of Obi-Wan hanging on to the assassin droid, which would be a CG character, were captured at Elstree Studios in England, where production moved after its location shoot in the last days of the principal photography schedule. Convenience, logistics, and cost-savings dictated the move; but there were sentimental reasons for it, as well—Elstree, which had hosted the original Star Wars productions, was considered by the filmmakers to be their "home" in London.

O n the bluescreen stage at Elstree, Ewan McGregor hung from a blue-covered crane arm as a giant fan blew back his hair and clothing to create the illusion of movement for shots of Obi-Wan hanging on to the flying droid. The computer-animated droid and digital backgrounds whizzing past at high speed were inserted into the bluescreen area by ILM.

When Zam takes a shot at the flying Jedi Knight from an upper-story alcove, the droid explodes into pieces, and Obi-Wan drops dozens of stories before being caught by an airspeeder piloted by Anakin. The airspeeders—both Anakin's and, seen later, Zam's—were among the vehicles developed by the concept design department. Inspiration for the speeders came from race car models Lucas had in his possession and from the *American Graffiti* director's long-standing interest in fast cars. "I was fascinated with these models," Lucas recalled. "I told Doug Chiang to take the top half of one car and the bottom of another car and splice them together—and that's how we created the speeders. Anakin's speeder was the most like a hot rod, with exposed engines in the front."

For shots of the characters piloting the speeders, the production model shop, under the direction of model making superviser Peter Wyborn, built ship interiors that were mounted to gimbals as a means of executing banking and rolling movements against a bluescreen backdrop. "Both the interiors and exteriors of the speeders had a kind of 1960s look," Wyborn noted. "In fact, the interiors looked like a Studebaker Superhawk. All the ships were very much like big cars from that time, which made them a great deal of fun to dress."

A long and complex action sequence through the night skies of Coruscant, the airspeeder chase had been thoroughly choreographed long before the start of principal photography. Editor and sound designer Ben Burtt, a long-time *Star Wars* veteran, had produced a series of "video-matics" for the sequence, made up of concept art, video footage he had shot—using his costumed son or Lucasfilm staffers as actors—vintage film clips, and stock footage.

"We have a bank of images we've collected over the years," Burtt said. "I started putting those together, along with video footage, just to give us an idea of what was

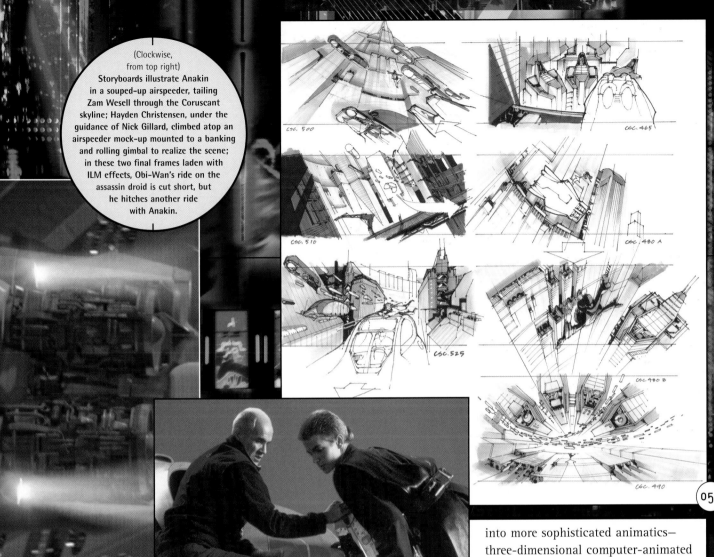

(Clockwise, from top right) Storyboards illustrate Anakin in a souped-up airspeeder, tailing Zam Wesell through the Coruscant skyline; Hayden Christensen, under the guidance of Nick Gillard, climbed atop an airspeeder mock-up mounted to a banking and rolling gimbal to realize the scene; in these two final frames laden with ILM effects, Obi-Wan's ride on the assassin droid is cut short, but he hitches another ride with Anakin.

CSC. 500
CSC. 465
CSC. 510
CSC. 480 A
CSC. 525
CSC. 480 B
CSC. 490

going to happen in the sequence. It was a Saturday-morning-cartoon version of the speeder chase that illustrated what they needed to shoot on stage. It gave everyone a sense of the scene—how many shots does it take to tell this part of the story, and within each shot, what is the action? What is the camera position? It was also helpful for the art department, because it told them what they needed to build. Did they need to build the whole speeder or just the cockpit? Was the camera going to see it from the bottom or only from the front and top? All of that was worked out beforehand. Of course, George wasn't locked into that, and he always gets new ideas once he gets to the set— but the videomatics were a start."

orking at the Ranch Main House, previsualization/ effects supervisor David Dozoretz and a team of four digital artists translated those videomatics into more sophisticated animatics— three-dimensional computer-animated shots that served as moving storyboards. "We started about two months before principal photography," Dozoretz recalled, "and right away, George gave us the speeder chase to work on. We knew the action for the speeder chase well enough to come up with a very rough cut of the sequence, because Ben Burtt worked with us before he left for Australia. We previsualized the entire thing before they ever went to shoot."

Over two and a half days of bluescreen filming for the sequence in Sydney, the animatics were played back on large plasma screens in front of McGregor and Christensen, seated in the gimbal-mounted airspeeder mock-ups. As cameras rolled, the actors would watch the screens and mimic the actions in the animatics, ducking signs when the animatic characters ducked, dodging debris and gunfire when the animatic characters dodged, et cetera. "The animatics for the speeder chase were very well developed," Ewan McGregor noted. "On Episode I, they were just basic shapes that gave us a rough idea of what was going on. But the animatics for Episode II looked great."

Lucas wanted the airspeeder chase to feature a number of distinctive Coruscant districts. In the final sequence, the chase moves from the high-rent "heights," through a warehouse district, and the "old" city (above and below) through an industrial area (opposite page), and finally to a seedy entertainment district.

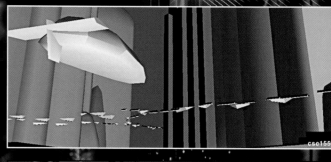

(Right)
Animatics enabled
Lucas to work out the
entire choreography and
action of the dynamic airspeeder
chase sequence prior to filming
its live-action elements in Sydney.
(Below) For clarification, the
visual effects team provided
a map of the chase
route.

The animatics were, in fact, highly detailed, showing the speeders flying through the cityscape of Coruscant, moving in and out of shadow and light, all of which provided clues as to how the actors and airspeeder mock-ups should be lit on stage. "The art department produced a map of the chase route," David Tattersall explained. "From that we could see the various situations the speeders went through during the chase—where they came close to buildings, or went through an industrial plant with lightning strike machines, or flew by fireballs or explosions. So there was a lot of potential for creating interactive light, and the animatics told us what we needed, lighting-wise, for specific parts of the chase."

Adjacent to the airspeeder-gimbal setup, a team of electricians installed interactive lighting rigs, such as a horseshoe-shaped overhead pulley system that moved a 5K lamp from one end of the horseshoe to the other, creating the illusion of the vehicles banking. There were also several motorized mirror boxes spinning around in front of the gimbal, as well as rows of lights on a sequential dimmer that traveled up and down the side of the vehicles to suggest high speed. Some or all of the lighting rigs were put into

service as Lucas shot one-and-a-half- to two-minute-long segments of the chase at a time.

The gimbal was designed and built by special effects supervisor Dave Young. "They wanted extreme movement for these ships," Young recalled, "so I designed a gimbal that could do a one-hundred-ninety-degree roll, twenty-five degrees of pitch, and sixty degrees on either side of center for the yaw. We could do all this at high speed, while going up and down, and moving along a meter-long track. This thing gave the actors something to react to inside the speeders. It

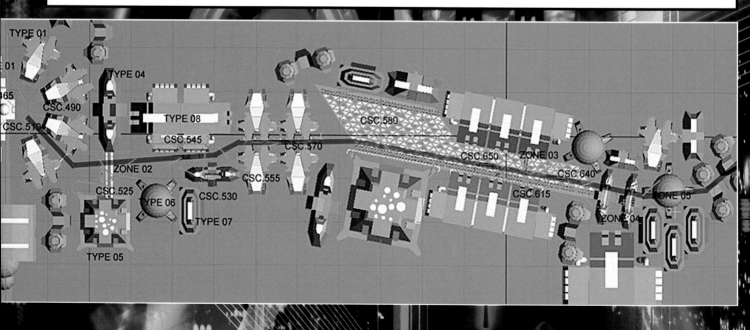

TYPE 01

01

65

CSC.490

CSC.510

TYPE 04

TYPE 08

CSC.545

CSC.570

CSC.580

CSC.650 ZONE 03

CSC.640

ZONE 02

CSC.555

CSC.615

ZONE 05

CSC.525

TYPE 06

CSC.530

TYPE 07

ZONE 04

TYPE 05

Final airspeeder-chase images combined computer-generated vehicles—the designs of which were based on 1950s-era hot-rod models—with ILM's CG and miniature environments. To get the biggest bang out of their CG buck, the visual effects crew built a limited number of 3D buildings, then expanded their number by mixing and matching rooftops and other structural dressings.

059

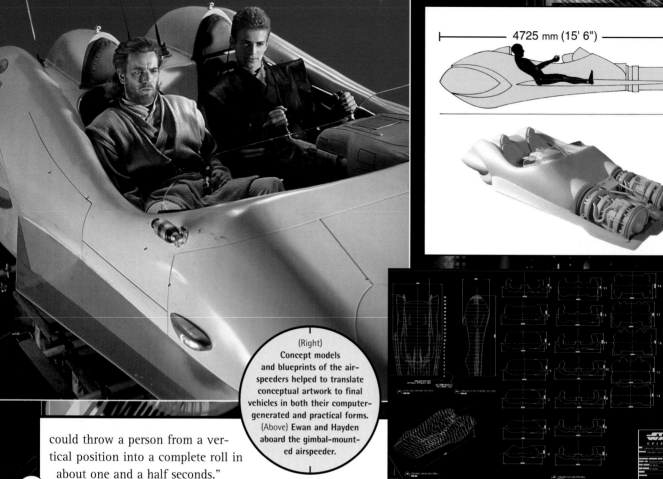

4725 mm (15' 6")

(Right)
Concept models
and blueprints of the airspeeders helped to translate
conceptual artwork to final
vehicles in both their computer-
generated and practical forms.
(Above) Ewan and Hayden
aboard the gimbal-mount-
ed airspeeder.

could throw a person from a ver-
tical position into a complete roll in
about one and a half seconds."

McGregor and Christensen spent many hours on the
"E-ticket" ride as Lucas captured live-action elements for
the speeder chase. "It actually made us feel rather sick after
a while," McGregor recalled. "It was like going on a fair-
ground ride over and over again—you're not even allowed
to have a hot dog, you've just got to keep doing it. It looked
like fun, but it was really a sick-making experience."

At one point in the chase, Anakin jumps from his
own airspeeder to Zam's far below him, gamely holding on
as the assassin banks and accelerates in an attempt to lose
her unwelcome passenger. Christensen spent a day crawling
around the gimbal-mounted speeder, trying to hold on for
real as it pitched and rolled. "That was a tough day,"
Christensen recalled. "I was being thrown around, trying to
hold on to this thing and climbing all over it. I felt like a
bit of an ass as I was doing it, but they said it would all
work out, and I trusted them. The cool thing was just
getting into this speeder. It was like going back to being
an eight-year-old kid!"

Added to those live-action elements many months
later were digital sets whizzing past in the background, digital speeders for exterior shots, and the sound of muscle car
engines, incorporated into the sound mix by supervising
sound editors Ben Burtt and Matthew Wood. "The way the
speeders were designed," Burtt said, "they looked like GTOs
or Mustangs. There were a couple of shots in that sequence
that looked as if they came right out of *American Graffiti*,
complete with tail fins and headlights. We had to develop
sounds that complemented the idea of hot rods in space."

The chase ends when Zam's compromised airspeeder
crashes onto an entertainment street in front of a seedy
Coruscant dive, the Outlander gambling club. Though the
crash was a digital effect, its immediate aftermath was captured live on stage with a practical speeder and 150 extras
in costumes and masks. For this scene and others, creatures
supervisor Jason Baird oversaw the use of hundreds of
character masks, some fabricated from scratch, others—
including those from the cantina scene in the original *Star
Wars*—pulled from the Lucasfilm archives and refurbished.

Gavin Bocquet's team built one main street, then
revamped that in a two-day changeover, changing
the dressings and colors to create an alleyway
for a later scene outside the club. Wide views were supplied
by ILM through CG set extensions and a street miniature.
"Because there was so much more matte painting work
on this film than there was on Episode I," John Knoll
explained, "I steered some of the set extensions that could
have been done as digital matte paintings toward miniatures. If I could do a shot with a miniature, I always went
that way—in part because we didn't have enough matte
department resources to complete the work. So the model
shop did a lot of work that, under other circumstances,

In their workshop in Sydney, members of Bocquet's construction crew assembled a full-size airspeeder mock-up of Zam's airspeeder, used for live-action shots of the characters within the cockpits. Because the mock-up would have to rock and roll on a motion gimbal, the crew built it out of lightweight materials.

felt a little better after that. And the further we got into the schedule, the more they understood what we were doing with the bluescreen." Closely followed by Obi-Wan and Anakin, Zam Wesell runs from the crash scene and into the crowded club, where dozens of aliens drink, mingle, play games, and bet on Podraces and other sports events broadcast on large screens.

might have been matte paintings. For these street shots, we built many little building fronts and moved those around to cover most of our Coruscant street extensions. Then, way in the background, where you see out to distant landscapes, we used matte paintings."

The practical set built on stage in Sydney was small, surrounded on all sides and at the top with bluescreen to enable ILM to complete the street scene in postproduction. For members of the crew who hadn't previously worked on such an effects-heavy production—which included most of them—the preponderance of blue was somewhat disorienting.

"The new crew members had something of a meltdown that day," McCallum recalled. "They just couldn't conceive how it was all going to turn out, and there was a lot of dismay. So I had to give them a little pep talk. I said: 'Look, guys, let me tell you what is going to be here that you don't see right now. There are going to be hundreds of aircraft and speeders flying by. There are going to be skyscrapers that reach up five, six hundred stories. There will be subway trains, hundreds of people, thousands of lights.' I think they

Bocquet's art department supplied concepts for the club interior, based on information gleaned from Lucas. "We weren't quite sure, in the beginning, what direction George wanted to go in for that scene," Bocquet recalled, "whether he wanted this to be a seedy bar, or a glitzy nightclub. We knew that he wanted it to be much bigger and more high-tech than the cantina in the first movie, so our concepts reflected that, with big raised platforms, walkways, and balconies. We showed George three models, each of which was a different style, and he chose a circular design. He ripped pieces off the model and moved them around— 'Why don't we have this here and this here?' We've learned to make our models completely detachable because he likes to do that. Then he signed off on this quite simple conceptual model, rather than having us redo it in a larger scale.

"We built the full-sized set from that small model and, consequently, I was always nervous about showing him this

(Clockwise from right) Rendering by Marc Gabbana for the exterior entrance to the Outlander, the gambling club into which Obi-Wan and Anakin pursue Zam; the entrance was represented by set models built by Gavin Bocquet's group, one of which bears reference letters; photography of the ILM miniature would eventually be combined with bluescreen footage of Obi-Wan and Anakin for a brief scene in front of the flashy establishment.

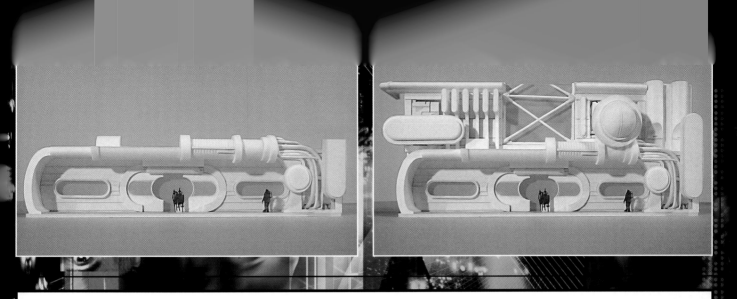

set. The model was at such a small scale, the immense size of this set wasn't necessarily apparent. In fact, we actually built the set twenty percent smaller than the model without telling George, because I was sure it would be too big once it was scaled up. And it is a good thing we did that, because even as it was, when he walked in a week before shooting and saw how large the set was, he said:

BUILDING 3
BAR SIDE
ENTRANCE

BUILDING 1 - BAR ENTRANCE

D

B

BUILDING 4

BUILDING 2

A

BUILDING 5

'Oh! I didn't realize it was going to be this big.' That set filled Stage Three, which was a hundred and twenty feet square. It was the cantina scene times twenty, with all these amazing characters running around in masks and costumes."

The final set measured seventy feet in diameter and featured high-tech droid drink dispensers, holographic gaming

tables, and gaming machines furnished by Peter Walpole. "The gaming machines were actually made out of two flotation devices off a seaplane, which we got from an aircraft parts dealer in Sydney," Walpole explained. "We also got some ordinary arcade games—like racing games that you sit in—and we cut them up a little bit, turned them upside down, and put them in the background." The completed set was resplendent with neon signs, flashing lights, tubes filled with glowing, gelatinous liquids, and backlit panels illuminated through custom-built strips of forty-watt, golf-ball-sized bulbs. Seven thousand bulbs were ultimately used on the set to create the appropriate ambient lighting.

When it came time to shoot the club scene, Lucas took full advantage of the spacious set, devising camera moves that would show it to its best advantage. "Although George felt it was a bit oversized for the scene," Bocquet said, "once he got used to the space, he was very excited about what he could do on it. He wound up doing a very large crane shot coming in from the door, revealing the whole of the environment. Overall, I think George moved the camera more dynamically on this movie than he did on Episode I."

One of the reasons for that more dynamic camera movement was Lucas's employment of the Technocrane, a relatively new piece of moviemaking equipment. "George had never really been into cranes," Rick McCallum explained. "He likes more conventional ways of shooting, and in the past cranes have been cumbersome and hard to deal with, requiring their own special crane crew. However, on this movie, I made sure George had a Technocrane, just because I love them. Our Australian operators, who knew that crane better than anybody, showed George what he could do with it, and I could see on his face how excited he was. Originally, I'd only booked the crane for the first day of shooting, for a high-angle shot on the Senate Hall set; but we wound up keeping it throughout the rest of the shoot, and George used it all the time. He absolutely loved it. He was a bit like a little boy with his first Lego!"

A set model by Bocquet's group of the interior of the Outlander club. Except for a small betting room off to the side of the bar that was a digital construction, Gavin Bocquet's crew built the entire club interior as a full-size set. (Right) The set, which filled the 120-square-foot Stage Three in Sydney, featured high-tech droid drink dispensers and gaming machines created from airplane scrap and modified arcade units by set decorator Peter Walpole and his crew.

T he club scene was shot on July 17, 2000. Makeup calls that day began at 2 A.M. for the approximately two hundred nightclub patrons—some human-looking, some in creature masks—played by local and near-local extras, cast by Rick McCallum from Sydney, New Zealand, Fiji, and Samoa over a two-week period. Final selections were made by Lucas, who reviewed photographs of the potential clubbers. The extras had been fitted for their costumes weeks before, but final adjustments were made the day of the shoot, a logistical nightmare due to the sheer numbers involved. In addition, all two hundred performers had to have their makeup and hair done—in often outrageous styles—requiring a hair and makeup crew of twenty-five, and rows of makeup/hair stations with mirrors.

From the principal actors' standpoint, performing within a complete set and with live characters was a welcome change from the more typical partial set surrounded by blue-screen. "The club scene was a lot of fun," Hayden Christensen

The production team costumed, masked, and made up two hundred extras from Sydney and nearby regions to fill the massive set with *Star Wars*–style patrons.

confirmed. "Usually we were just in a sea of blue, not really knowing what we were supposed to be looking at. But this was an actual set, with a lot of extras walking around that we could react to and play off of."

Patrons included not only Lucas's daughters, Katie and Amanda, but also Ahmed Best, droid unit supervisor Don Bies, and Anthony Daniels in his first *Star Wars* appearance outside his C-3PO costume. Bies played a pumped-up, macho outer-space man; Best portrayed Achk Med-Beq, a

Bocquet's blueprints for the gambling club interior set. Referring to the bar featured in the original Star Wars, Bocquet described the set as "the cantina, times twenty." Bocquet initially presented Lucas with three club models from which to choose. Lucas approved the circular design, but rearranged its layout by breaking off structural features and moving them around.

july 17, 2000
fox studios, sydney

Extras wearing exotic hairstyles and costumes await their call outside Stage 2, where the art department has erected a gambling club—*Star Wars*-style—for a scene in which Obi-Wan and Anakin go in search of assassin Zam Wesell. Dozens of masked, made-up, and costumed extras are already on set, receiving instructions from assistant directors (A.D.). Two women are sent to a stylized chesslike game table; another group is sent to huddle over a bizarre "card and dice" game.

"I have no idea what game this is supposed to be," the assistant director admits, looking at the game table and shaking his head.

"We were told it was like craps," one extra offers.

The A.D. shrugs. "Okay...I guess it could be that. You, you're the dealer; the rest of you are playing."

Among the nightclub patrons are Anthony Daniels and Ahmed Best, playing an "officer" and a gambler, respectively. Chatting with the extras, Daniels recounts a story of shooting the cantina scene for the first *Star Wars*.

"We came in, and the actor playing the bartender said, 'Get those *druids* out of here,'" Daniels recalls, "instead of 'No droids allowed.'" As the extras laugh, Lucas approaches Daniels.

"Come with me," he says. "We're going to fix you up with a date." Daniels is delighted—until Lucas introduces him to a grotesque, scaly, masked creature. "Meet Judy."

"After all these years," Daniels protests, laughing, "*this* is what you give me!"

With the appearance on set of Hayden Christensen and Ewan McGregor, Lucas rehearses a shot of Anakin and Obi-Wan entering the bar. Christensen is impressed with the set *and* its inhabitants. "It's fantastic," he says to Lucas. "And cute girls everywhere! It's a little distracting..." He smiles as he looks around the room.

Later in the day, the company moves on to a scene in which Zam sneaks up on Obi-Wan at the bar, blaster drawn. At the last moment, Obi-Wan spins in his seat and severs the bounty hunter's forearm with his lightsaber.

Lucas walks through the action with the actors and his assistant directors. "How shall we cue Ewan at the bar?" one asks, meaning how will McGregor know when actress Leeanna Walsman, as Zam, is directly behind him. Lucas suggests simply yelling out the actor's name at the appropriate moment.

During rehearsal, the extras jump enthusiastically into their assigned activities—some playing games, some dancing. Walsman approaches the bar. McGregor's name is called. He spins around, lightsaber in hand, and strikes. Walsman falls to the ground.

Appearing for the first time outside his C-3PO suit in a Star Wars film, Anthony Daniels (left) portrayed con man Danni Faytonni in the nightclub scene. Daniels chats with Leeanna Walsman (Zam without her mask, right) and Matt Doran (Elan Sleazebaggano, middle) between shots.

"Cut."

Just before the next rehearsal, an A.D. instructs the dancing extras to be a bit more animated. "You're in a funky nightclub, folks. Let's make it look like you are!"

His direction is taken to heart, and the energy level is much higher among the extras the second time through. It is, in fact, a bit *too* high. "You know," Lucas says to first A.D. James McTeigue, "it's just a *bar.* I'm not even sure if there is going to be music—and some of them are going nuts with the dancing."

McTeigue smiles, understanding the extras' overeagerness to please. "We'll tone that down a bit," he assures Lucas.

(Above)
Ahmed Best (Jar Jar Binks) also appeared for the first time without digital enhancements as Achk Med-Beq, another con man, shown here with Jenna Greene (Lunae Minx). (Below) Obi-Wan refuses a death-stick from "pusher" Elan Sleazebaggano; a few moments later, stalked by Zam Wesell, Obi-Wan whips around and severs her arm with his lightsaber; in an adjacent alleyway, Obi-Wan and Anakin question Zam.

gambling patron; and Daniels played a Corellian, "Lieutenant" Danni Faytonni. "I have been in five *Star Wars* movies now," Daniels noted, "but never as a person! It was great to play this officer, drinking with his friends. I had a soft and pliable costume that I could sit down in, and I could use my hands properly and even pick things up!"

067

Many of the younger extras didn't recognize Daniels and were curious as to why he seemed to know everyone on the crew. "I explained my previous involvement," Daniels recalled, "going back twenty-four years to when I first entered the original cantina. It was weird to be back in a similar set all these years later, but it was a great day with a great party atmosphere."

Ahmed Best also found the experience exhilarating. "I finally got my face on screen!" he exclaimed. "It was a long day, about thirteen hours, and I was on my feet throughout; but I did it for the prestige of being on camera."

As Anakin searches the perimeter of the establishment, Obi-Wan sits at the bar, presumably to have a drink. Zam Wesell emerges stealthily from the crowd, blaster drawn, and points the weapon at his back. The prop department provided the blaster and all the weapons carried by the club patrons, fabricating three thousand weapons in total for the film. Prototypes were first built in aluminum, then prop versions were cast in resin and fiberglass.

(Clockwise from middle left) **An animatics representation of a spaceport and the space freighter; the same elements as they were seen in the final film; after viewing a first cut of the movie, Lucas added a new scene between Anakin and Palpatine to more firmly establish the bond between them (because the office set was no longer standing, bluescreen elements of Christensen and McDiarmid were inserted into office footage already shot for other scenes); a model of the space freighter built by concept model maker John Goodson.**

Suddenly, in a move reminiscent of his action in the Mos Eisley bar in *Star Wars: A New Hope*, Obi-Wan spins in his seat, lightsaber in hand, and cuts off his adversary's forearm. Zam falls, then Obi-Wan and Anakin carry her to an alley outside the club where she is about to reveal the name of the person who hired her to kill Padmé. Before the name is uttered, she is shot with a toxic dart by a rocket-man—actually Jango Fett—her form changing back to that of an alien Clawdite as she dies. The transition from actress to alien was an ILM computer effect.

W ith this latest assassination attempt, the Jedi Council decides that Padmé must go into hiding, with Anakin as her protector, while Obi-Wan investigates the origins of the toxic dart. To enlist his help in persuading Padmé, the Council suggests that Anakin

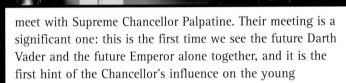

meet with Supreme Chancellor Palpatine. Their meeting is a significant one: this is the first time we see the future Darth Vader and the future Emperor alone together, and it is the first hint of the Chancellor's influence on the young

Anakin. Not included in the original script, the scene was added by Lucas after he assembled the first cut of the film, and was shot during the fall 2001 pickups at Ealing Studios.

"In the original script, there were subtle inferences that there was some kind of relationship between Anakin and Palpatine," Lucas said. "There was dialogue where Anakin said he thought Palpatine was a good Chancellor and not like other politicians, so it was obvious that he knew him. But when I saw the first cut of the movie, I realized that we needed to push that point harder. As it was, the inferences were a bit *too* subtle.

"Although the relationship between Anakin and Palpatine doesn't really relate to this movie—it's more important to the next movie—I had to set that up because it was important in the overall arc of the story. So I wrote that little scene to show Palpatine's influence on Anakin and his role as mentor." Rather than rebuild the Palpatine office set on the Ealing stages, the filmmakers employed shots of the office that had already been filmed for other scenes. "We took those shots of the office and digitally erased all the people in them, and then plugged in the bluescreen elements of Anakin and Palpatine that we shot at Ealing."

Convinced of the danger of staying on Coruscant, Anakin and Padmé, disguised in peasant garb, arrive at a bustling spaceport and enter the bowels of a space freighter bound for Naboo. Establishing shots were computer-generated, but a space freighter interior set was built for the live-action scenes, its look based on the steerage class of an ocean liner like the *Titanic*.

"Gavin designed that set with bunk beds down one side and a center section for cargo," Peter Walpole explained. "Then, on the other side, there was a small cafeteria. We also made camp beds on the floor where refugees might sleep in this overcrowded hold. It was all sort of dark and gloomy." Scenes within the star freighter were filmed early in the fourth week of production.

(Below)
Although exterior shots of the freighter were all computer-generated, Gavin Bocquet's group built a freighter interior set for live-action scenes, basing its design on the steerage class of an ocean liner. (Right and above) A set model and a rough 3D computer rendering of the freighter interior.

(Above)
Lucas on the set with Natalie Portman as Padmé and Rose Byrne (left) as her handmaiden Dormé. (Right) Trisha Biggar's peasant costume for Padmé included an intricate headdress. Every effort was made to keep all the headpieces as lightweight as possible to ensure Portman's comfort during long shooting days. (Below) The crew prepares to shoot a space freighter interior scene that was ultimately cut from the film for purposes of pacing.

As part of her peasant disguise, Padmé wears one of her most elaborate headdresses. "It looked almost like wicker-work," Ivo Coveney noted. "We made a framework of piano wire that George liked, and then we wove in strips of styrene. We had to make sure it was as lightweight as possible, because Natalie was going to be wearing it all day. In fact, that was a major consideration with all of the headdresses. I teased Natalie a bit, telling her that I'd read some of her interviews after Episode I where she'd complained about how heavy and uncomfortable the headdresses were. I promised her we'd try to make them as light as possible this time."

"The headdresses *were* less painful this time," Portman admitted. "On this film, everybody was much more careful about that, making me as comfortable as possible since I had to act with these things on. It is difficult to concen-trate on acting when you're in pain! But they were still beautiful, and very much in the culture of *Star Wars*."

With the departure of Padmé and Anakin, Obi-Wan visits a diner owned and operated by his old friend Dexter Jettster, a vaguely amphibian-looking alien he hopes will recognize the markings and origin of the toxic dart that killed Zam Wesell. As Obi-Wan enters the establishment, he is waited on by a WA-7 droid on a unipod wheel, which echoes the roller-skating wait-resses of *American Graffiti.*

Indeed, the Dex's Diner set was designed to reflect the spirit of a real 1950s diner in general and the diner from *American Graffiti* in particular, but with high-tech flour-ishes that placed it firmly in the *Star Wars* galaxy.

(Left)
Computer-rendered views of Dexter's Diner, where Obi-Wan visits an old friend to determine the origins of the toxic dart that killed Zam Wesell. The diner was inspired by the one featured in Lucas's American Graffiti (1973). (Below) Models built by Bocquet's team.

The full-size diner set included red vinyl booths, a counter with bar stools, and a back kitchen area where fog machines mounted to the floor created rising steam on Lucas's cue. The production prop department created imaginative, bizarre alien foodstuffs—such as blue pastries and super-sized multidecker sandwiches—to dress the set. A crew member hangs a sign—inscribed with alien-style lettering—in the Dexter's Diner set.

(Above)
The exterior of
Dexter's Diner. Construction
crews built the diner and a small
street area on stage, extended
by ILM with miniatures and a digital
matte painting. (Below) Seen only
briefly through the order window,
the kitchen area of the diner
set was well stocked with the
appropriate pots, pans,
and appliances.

july 26, 2000
fox studios, sydney

The art department has erected a minimalistic set to represent the interior of Jango Fett's apartment on Kamino. The set's stark white shapes, black reflective surfaces, and chrome tubing are reminiscent of the original stormtrooper uniform—a deliberate aesthetic choice. Because the smooth, polished surfaces must remain free of scuff marks, a sign has been posted at the entrance: PLEASE USE BOOTIES PROVIDED WHEN WALKING ON SET. All of the crew members comply, going about their business with blue surgical booties over their shoes.

The crew is shooting Obi-Wan's arrival at the apartment, where he meets Jango's ten-year-old clone/son, Boba Fett, played by Daniel Logan. The action will be captured both from the inside of the apartment, where the cameras are currently stationed, and, in the next setup, from the exterior hallway. Logan waits for Lucas's cue on one side of a door, while Ewan McGregor stands on the other side, chewing gum.

On "Action," Logan touches a pad on the wall to open the door—actually operated from off-camera—and speaks to Obi-Wan and his Kaminoan companion, Taun We. Actress Rena Owen, who will do the voice for the digital Kaminoan, stands in during this rehearsal. To ensure proper eyelines, she wears a hard hat to which a cardboard cutout of Taun We's long neck and head has been attached, adding several feet to her actual height. When the actors go through the scene again, Owen performs her lines off-camera.

The next setup is from the hallway, and cameras and lights are moved accordingly. Makeup personnel touch up Logan's face as he talks excitedly about "Billy the Bass"—a singing, animatronic fish that is this year's "Pet Rock." "Have you seen it?" he asks crew members, all of whom shake their heads no. "Catch me in the morning," Logan sings—one of the songs in Billy the Bass's repertoire. "I can't get that song out of my head!"

When the lights and cameras are in position, Lucas shoots the encounter between Obi-Wan and Boba at the door. Between takes, he instructs Logan to look at Obi-Wan with a bit more suspicion the next time through. As Lucas moves to his position at a monitor, McGregor leans down and whispers something to the boy, and the two of them begin to giggle.

The actors get control of themselves and they do the scene again. The door opens, and Boba looks at Obi-Wan with *intense* suspicion and distaste. Lucas calls "Cut," and strolls over to Logan. "Not *quite* so much of a look this time," he suggests gently.

Logan begins giggling again, pointing an accusing finger at McGregor. "Ewan told me to look at him as if he'd let off a really smelly fart!" the boy explains—

(Above) Jango Fett (Temuera Morrison) verbally spars with Obi-Wan. (Left) Daniel Logan as Boba Fett, the cloned son of Jango—and a future villain—experiences a lighter moment aboard Slave I.

although, in his New Zealand accent, the word comes out *faaht*, making it, somehow, more dignified.

The crew laughs, and McGregor shrugs, smiling innocently. "I thought it was a great note," he says.

"Okay," says Lucas, laughing, "but a little *less* smelly this time."

They do the scene one more time, perfectly; then Daniel Logan leaves for the day—out of makeup and costume, wearing a Darth Maul T-shirt.

075

SW2 CAFÉ DROID
WARREN FU
08 · 10 · 2000
005W

The WA-7 droid waitress in the final scene (above) and in conceptual form by visual effects concept artist Warren Fu (left). The droid was inspired by the roller-skating waitresses in Lucas's *American Graffiti* (1973).

076

Appearing from behind the kitchen doors, Dexter greets Obi-Wan with a warm bear hug, then hitches up his pants and squeezes his ample form into a red vinyl booth. Dexter instantly recognizes the toxic instrument as a saberdart from Kamino, a distant planet populated by cloners. When shooting rehearsals of the scene, actor Ronald Falk—who would perform the voice of Dexter—stood in for the CG character, allowing Ewan McGregor to obtain a sense of interaction before playing the scene to empty air. "We always try to have the voice actor on the set," Lucas explained, "doing the dialogue and playing the part. We shoot a couple of takes with the actor in the scene, and then we do a bunch of takes without the actor there to give us a clean plate."

One of the advantages of filming scenes with the voice actor present was that it provided invaluable reference for the computer animators. "I use those takes to see what the voice actor brought to the physical performance," Rob Coleman explained. "Unconsciously, an actor will do things with his head and hands as he is performing—even though he knows it's just a reference take—and if we incorporate those things into the computer-generated character, it makes our animation look much better. The voice actor for Dex helped us a great deal when it came time to animate that CG character. Falk was a great performer, and he was clearly having a lot of fun acting in the scene."

The CG Dex, built by ILM digital modeling supervisor Geoff Campbell and his team, was a massive character with four undulating arms, a scaly hide, and a hard shell at the top of his head; but the model also included recognizable facial features. "We've learned through the years that no matter how strange a character is, audiences have to be

"George understands how important it is to give people something to relate to in these bizarre environments," Bocquet noted. "So even though we were on Coruscant, we had a diner that looked like a diner as we know it. It would have looked perfectly in place in downtown Los Angeles—but put a few aliens and droid waitresses in it, and you're on Coruscant."

(Top) Ewan McGregor and voice actor Ron Falk (Dexter Jettster) run the diner scene. Filming the scene with the voice actor present gave McGregor a sense of interaction with the computer-generated Dex and provided ILM animators with invaluable performance cues for the completed scene (bottom).

able to connect to a face of some kind," Coleman said. "So Dex had two eyes, a nose, and a wide mouth. We also gave him a bum leg so he would walk with a limp, just to add some character to his movement."

An observant movie goer will spot CG alien species from Episode I sitting in the diner's background booths. Among them are Bogs Tyrell, a relative of Podracer Rats Tyrell, and Soboca, a Dug from Malastare like the Podracer Sebulba. With so many CG characters populating the scene, the live-action set was half-empty during filming, except for the presence of Ewan McGregor. "I kept the positions of all the CG characters in my head while I was shooting," Lucas recalled. "There was a waitress moving through the scene, and sometimes, to help us keep things straight, we'd use a real waitress, even though we thought she might be replaced with a CG robot."

A rmed with Dexter's information regarding the toxic dart, Obi-Wan goes to the Jedi Temple Archives to research the planet Kamino. The establishing shot of the Jedi Temple was a combination of digital matte paintings and a tower miniature, first built and shot for Episode I, which was photographed from a different angle to give it a slightly altered appearance.

The character maquette for Dexter, as sculpted by model maker Murnane. The maquette was scanned into the computer by the digital modelers at ILM to provide a starting point for the building of the computer-generated character.

Episode II would feature more interiors of the Jedi Temple than the previous film—not only the archives room and main council chamber, but also Mace Windu's office and a variety of corridors. The interiors were created primarily through 3D digital sets, matte paintings, or miniatures, with the art department providing only foreground columns and a textured floor upon which the actors would walk during live-action filming. Many of the interiors were simply revamped versions of the Jedi Council chamber set, re-dressed with new colors, furnishings, and architectural details. "We thought that, since all these rooms were in the same building, they could be more or less the same, structurally," Bocquet explained. "So we used that one set for four different rooms in the temple. By doing a clever bit of design work and dressing, we changed them enough so that, hopefully, the audience will never realize that they are all in the same set."

Lucas added yet another temple scene, long after principal photography had wrapped and long after the temple interior sets had been destroyed. "We realized we needed the 'chalkboard scene' that every movie has," he said, "where somebody sits down and says, 'This is what the movie is about, this is what has happened, and this is what is going

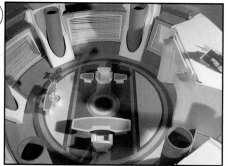

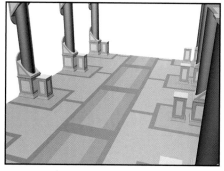

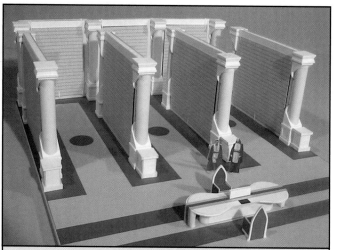

The library—shown here in computer renderings and set models created by Bocquet's team—was a partial live-action set, expanded with a miniature built and shot at ILM. ILM also provided computer graphics displays on archive monitors.

to happen.' We needed one of those between Yoda and Mace inside the temple, so I wrote it and we scheduled to shoot it at Ealing in March. But I didn't want to build a new Jedi Temple interior just for that one scene, so I decided to steal one from *The Phantom Menace.*

"We'd built a number of temple interiors for *The Phantom Menace* because there were several scenes set there—a scene with Qui-Gon Jinn and Obi-Wan, and another where Anakin is tested. We took all the shots from one of those scenes, erased Qui-Gon and Obi-Wan, and put in Yoda and Mace. We ended up with a filmed set in the middle of a digital movie—the *only* film in the movie, in fact. That set had been shot on film four years ago, but it cut in just fine."

Initially, the archives scene in the Jedi Temple had included a long dialogue between Obi-Wan and librarian Jocasta Nu (Alethea McGrath) in front of a statue of Count Dooku, during which much expository information about

the ex-Jedi was revealed. Lucas ultimately shortened the scene by half, excising all of the dialogue about Dooku. "We found that we didn't need that much exposition," Lucas stated. "There was some information about Qui-Gon Jinn having known Dooku, but now that comes out later in

a prison scene between Obi-Wan and Dooku. All of the other information wasn't that important anyway, so we took it out." Still in the scene, however, was a quick shot of Lucas's then seven-year-old son, Jett, as a Jedi learner who walks in and seeks the librarian's assistance.

C uriously, Obi-Wan's search of the archive charts reveals no record of the Kamino system. Consulting Yoda on the veranda where the old Master trains preschool-aged Jedi younglings, Obi-Wan

receives an answer out of the mouths of babes, who suggest that the archive maps have been altered to exclude Kamino. The very young Jedi-in-training were cast from dozens of local children—ranging in age from three to six years—who were auditioned by extras casting director Ros Breden. Stunt coordinator Nick Gillard was also instrumental in the casting decisions, because he was responsible for teaching the youngsters basic fencing moves with baby-sized lightsabers.

"All the kids were so great," Gillard said, "it was hard to turn any of them down." Fifteen children were finally chosen. "They were very good," Ewan McGregor recalled. "They all stood on their spots, didn't move about. Ahmed Best helped to keep them in line, and he was just fantastic with them."

079

(Above) Local Sydney three- to six-year-olds were cast, then trained by Nick Gillard (left) to handle tot-sized lightsabers. (Right) The young Jedi in hair and wardrobe on the Sydney stage. Many of the children's heads were ultimately replaced with the computer-animated heads of baby aliens.

With Yoda's blessing, Obi-Wan heads for the Jedi hangar, boards his Delta-7 starfighter (in an added scene that appears on the DVD), and leaves Coruscant for Kamino, in search of an assassin.

He will find much, much more.

chapter
four

on Naboo

Anakin and Padmé arrive in Theed, Naboo's capital city, and make their way to the palace for an audience with Queen Jamillia, Padmé's successor to the throne. The pair is seen within the Theed Palace courtyard, which was shot near Seville, Spain, by the first unit near the end of principal photography. Temperatures soared to 120 degrees the day filming took place on a public square in the middle of town, with thousands of locals watching. Though production flew in for only one day of filming, then left the next morning, the location shoot had required ten weeks of preparation.

(Right)
Crew on the Plaza d'Espana, Seville, Spain.
(Below) Inspired by the picturesque plaza in Seville, pre-visualization/effects artist Simon Dunsdon created this animatic of Theed plaza.

We arrived on a chartered jet," Rick McCallum said, "and we had to be shooting an hour and a half later. It was like an army maneuver, setting up makeshift tents and all the equipment as quickly as we could." Among the mishaps that added to the chaos was a camera gear truck that broke down. Fortunately, a local truck passed by, and because the driver was an avid *Star Wars* fan, he offered his more than enthusiastic assistance.

Theed Palace interiors were shot within the eighteenth-century palace at Caserta, approximately twenty miles from Naples, Italy, just as they had been for *The Phantom Menace*. Partly in appreciation for the Australian crew's hard work during the stage shoot, and partly out of a desire for continuity, Rick McCallum arranged for the entire crew to travel to the location shoots—an unusual circumstance in the film industry. "It was important to give the crew a sense of closure—and they were willing to fly coach," McCallum joked. "Everyone was exhausted, but they took this thirty-five-hour flight to Italy, had a day off, and felt fantastic the next day."

Very little was required in the way of construction or dressing to augment Caserta's naturally elegant setting. Even the palace furniture from Episode I was available to production, because it had been kept in storage at Skywalker Ranch. "If I were a piece of furniture for Caserta," Peter Walpole observed, "I'd have a tremendous number of air miles! We shipped it from the Ranch to Australia to check it over and make sure it was okay; then we shipped it from Australia to Italy. We did end up having to rebuild a desk, but the throne chair and other things were still existing, and we just changed the upholstery to indicate a new Queen and the passage of time. But since it was a continuity set, George didn't want it changed too much from the first movie."

Due to the popularity of the palace as a tourist attraction, production was limited to shooting between the hours of 1 P.M. and 1 A.M. on its one and only day there. Another restriction was that no piece of lighting or camera equipment could be mounted to or even *touch* the walls or ceilings. "Those regulations compromised our ability to light things exactly as we wanted," David Tattersall observed. "Since we couldn't hang any lights, we used helium balloons filled with lights to

083

George Lucas greets enthusiastic onlookers and autograph seekers on location in Spain.

Doug Chiang replaced Seville's existing architectural features with Naboo's characteristic domes.

(Right) **Ayesha Dharker**, whom Robin Gurland spotted in a little-known Indian film titled *The Terrorist*, played Queen Jamillia, Padmé's successor to the Naboo throne. (Below) Dharker's ceremonial costume included an elaborate headdress made up of mother-of-pearl petals.

illuminate those scenes. The balloons floated over the set, throwing a nice soft light on the whole thing."

The filming of the throne room scene was Ayesha Dharker's only day on the shoot. The Indian actress had been cast as Queen Jamillia through an unlikely series of coincidences. While auditioning actors for Anakin in New York, casting director Robin Gurland had read an article in *The New York Times*, written by John Malkovich, about a low-budget, virtually unknown Indian film titled *Malli*, which the actor had seen while serving as a juror at the Cairo Film Festival. "Malkovich had loved the film," Gurland said, "had taken it under his wing, and was promoting it. This article went on about the film's lead actress, Ayesha Dharker, and it had a tight shot of her. I thought, 'This woman looks amazing—I've got to see her for the Queen.' And so I made a note to track her down somehow."

Later that same day, Gurland met with Samuel Jackson, who was in town shooting *Shaft*, and mentioned to him this Indian film, renamed *The Terrorist* for its limited U.S. distribution. "Sam said, 'I have a copy of it,'" Gurland recalled. "'*What?*' Someone had

sent it to him because they wanted him to do this director's next film. He just walked over, pulled it down from his shelf, and said, 'Here, take it.' So I looked at the film that night, and I just fell in love with this girl. I finally tracked her down, met her in London—and, just like that, we cast her as the Queen."

Dharker's hair, makeup, and costuming mirrored those worn by Natalie Portman in Episode I: her face was covered in a white, ceremonial makeup, and she wore a very formal embroidered dress, set off with an elaborate headdress made up of eight seven-inch-tall mother-of-pearl petals. Construction of the headdress was extremely time-consuming, because the costume prop department had to fabricate 120 petals to arrive at eight that were a perfect color match.

The conference with the Queen results in the decision that Padmé go into hiding at a retreat in Naboo's Lake Country. Originally, what followed the throne room scene was one in which Padmé and Anakin visit her family in Theed before their departure. Featuring her father, mother, sister, and nieces, the scene had served to reveal a more personal side of Padmé. Lucas deleted the entire family reunion scene, however, after assembling his first cut of the film.

"It was nice to meet Padmé's family," Lucas commented, "but there wasn't really much relevant information provided by that scene. I had used the scene, initially, as a means of showing Padmé's parents putting some pressure on her to quit politics and settle down and start a family—at twenty-four years old, she was already quite late doing that, in Naboo terms. I thought that would help

august 2, 2000
fox studios, sydney

A stage has been transformed into a Tusken Raider camp. Anakin Skywalker will arrive there—too late—to rescue his mother from her captors. Because establishing views will be created through digital matte paintings and miniatures, only two mud huts have been built. A gas-controlled campfire burns between them. Sand strewn with rocks, animal bones, and other objects complete the set.

As cameras roll, George Lucas directs three performers portraying the Tusken Raiders standing guard outside the huts. "Talk to each other a bit," Lucas suggests. Then, pointing: "You, start to fall asleep; you, work on your gun."

Hayden Christensen arrives, and Lucas walks him through his actions. "Creep around the side here," he says, as he moves around one of the huts, "then over to here." He points to a spot on a muddy wall. "This is where you'll cut the hole." He's referring to the scripted action in which Anakin gains entrance to the hut by using his lightsaber to slice a hole in the wall—an effect that will be achieved through a combination of practical and digital pyrotechnics.

Lucas discusses the scene with special effects supervisor Dave Young. "I'm concerned how big the pyro effect is going to be," he says.

Christensen laughs at the thought. "Don't mind me," he jokes, as if talking to the Tusken guards, "I'm just sneaking in here."

When the crew is ready to shoot, Christensen is handed a prop lightsaber, and Lucas calls, "Action!" Christensen moves stealthily around the hut, then mimes cutting the hole into its side. With that clean version captured—a plate that will enable ILM to insert the necessary digital effects—Dave Young's crew attaches a ring of pyrotechnic charges around the prescored hole. The art department sprays black paint around the perimeter, giving it a scorched look.

They shoot the scene again, but this time, practical sparks fly and small flames ignite. Christensen puts

(Above) **Only two full-scale huts were built on stage for the filming of the scene in which Anakin finds his mother held captive in a Tusken Raider camp. Additional huts and backgrounds shown in wide shots were a combination of miniatures and digital matte paintings.** (Right) **Lucas speaks with Pernilla August (Shmi Skywalker) during the filming of one of the film's most intense scenes.**

his foot on the hut, as if to kick the piece through, and Lucas calls, "Cut."

The crew now prepares to shoot yet another version, in which the cut piece drops into the hut. Since the pyro was more cosmetic than functional, sections of the "cut" perimeter remain intact, and the crew must saw through them so that the piece will disengage cleanly.

Pernilla August, returning as Anakin's mother, Shmi, arrives on set, made up with cuts and bruises, and wearing a torn and tattered costume. She and Christensen exchange "good mornings," kissing the air at the sides of their cheeks to avoid smudging her carefully applied wounds.

The crew moves on to the scene between mother and son within the hut interior—a separate set, cut in half to allow camera access. A fire burns inside, casting eerie flickers of light on the actors' faces. When cameras roll, Christensen steps into the hut, then pulls August down from a wooden rack. The camera moves in tight on the intimate scene, which is both a reunion and a good-bye. Shmi dies. Anakin breaks down.

The quiet on the set is broken by Lucas's softly whispered, "Cut."

(Clockwise from left-hand page) **Lucas confers with Hayden** during scenes shot at Villa Balbaniello on Lake Como in northern Italy. Lucas had visited the estate while vacationing the previous year and had written all of the retreat scenes with the villa in mind; ILM matte painters modified the estate's exterior to reflect Naboo's domed architectural style; Villa Balbaniello as it actually appears.

Cast and crew brave the rainstorm that greeted them upon their arrival at the Villa Balbaniello. Lucas was forced to shoot in spurts, as the sun darted in and out of cloud cover. Production shot at the location for four days.

o88

motivate her relationship with Anakin. However, in watching the movie, I found that the love story worked fine without that element of pressure. The chemistry was there, and it was enough for her to fall in love with him. The parents scene was nice backstory, but it slowed down the movie unnecessarily."

(A)s finally cut together, the Naboo sequence moves from the audience with Queen Jamillia to a shot of a water speeder docking at a beautiful estate surrounded by lush gardens. All the exterior retreat scenes were filmed the first week of September 2000, during four days at Villa Balbaniello. The villa sits on the shores of Lake Como, one of the sites in northern Italy that Lucas had visited during his European vacation the previous year. "I went to Lake Como during my trip," Lucas recalled. "I'd been there before, but this time I walked around the Villa Balbaniello, and I thought it was fantastic. I knew I needed Anakin and Padmé to wind up at some romantic spot on

Naboo, and this was perfect. Once I saw it, I wrote all of those scenes with that location in mind."

The town of Como dates back to Roman times and still has an ancient quarter populated with medieval-era buildings, while the lakeshore features old world castles and villas with manicured grounds and gardens. Villa Balbaniello is one such estate. While its terraces and gardens were perfect for the retreat scenes, however, the architectural style of the actual structures wasn't entirely appropriate, so ILM digitally painted out some elements of the buildings and added other features. "We got rid of the turrets that were there," Rick McCallum explained, "and added digital matte paintings of the quintessential Naboo domes to the tops of the buildings. The funny thing is, even with those architectural changes, it is obvious in wide shots that this is Villa Balbaniello. If you've ever been there, if you know that place, you recognize it instantly."

In the intimacy of this beautiful lake setting, the long-standing affection between Anakin and Padmé blossoms into

(Clockwise from top) A location scouting shot of Villa Balbaniello seen from Lake Como; Lake Como seen from the villa; the production crew flanking one of the villa's statues; Concept artist Jay Shuster's color palette for the water speeder; Anakin and Padmé disembark from the constructed water speeder.

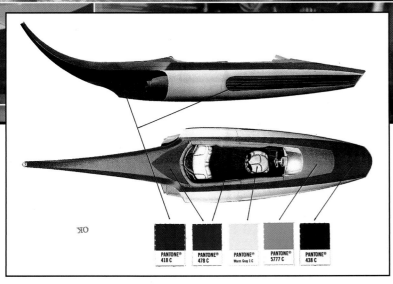

| PANTONE® 418 C | PANTONE® 478 C | PANTONE® Warm Gray 1 C | PANTONE® 5777 C | PANTONE® 438 C |

a deeply felt but forbidden love. Before writing a single word of the screenplay, George Lucas had known that the love story between Padmé and Anakin would be one of the most challenging aspects of this second episode in the *Star Wars* saga, demanding a different style of storytelling than that of the previous films.

"It wasn't that the writing of it was so difficult," Lucas explained. "I'd done a bit of writing a love story in *American Graffiti*, so writing wasn't the challenge. The challenge was that I wanted to tell the love story in a style that was extremely old-fashioned, and, frankly, I didn't know if I was going to be able to pull it off. In many ways, this was much more like a movie from the nineteen thirties than any of the others had been, with a slightly over-the-top, poetic style—and they just don't do that in movies anymore. I was very happy with the way it turned out in the script and in the performances, but I knew people might not buy it. A lot of guys were going to see this movie, and most guys think that kind of flowery, poetic talk is stupid—'Come on, give me a break.' More sophisticated, cynical types also don't buy that stuff. So I didn't know if people would laugh at it and throw things at the screen, or if they would accept it."

The delicate handling of the love scenes was required at every stage of production—from the writing, to the shooting, to the editing when Lucas returned to the Ranch and began cutting the film together with editor Ben Burtt. "There was a lot of chemistry between Natalie and Hayden,"

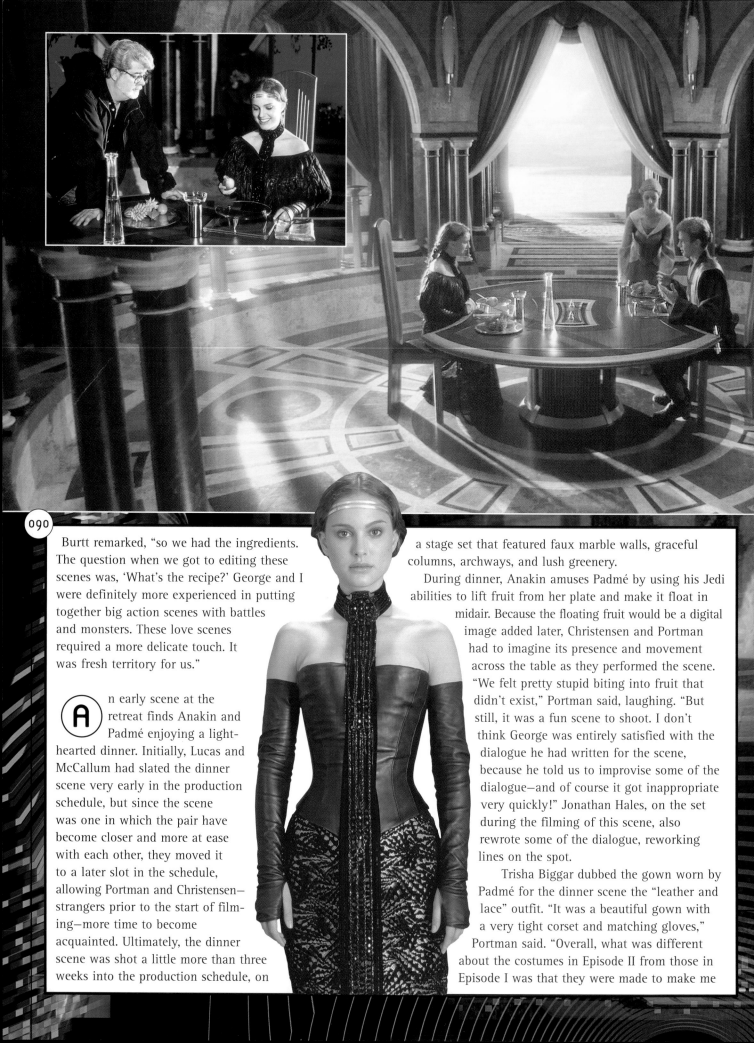

Burtt remarked, "so we had the ingredients. The question when we got to editing these scenes was, 'What's the recipe?' George and I were definitely more experienced in putting together big action scenes with battles and monsters. These love scenes required a more delicate touch. It was fresh territory for us."

Ⓐn early scene at the retreat finds Anakin and Padmé enjoying a light-hearted dinner. Initially, Lucas and McCallum had slated the dinner scene very early in the production schedule, but since the scene was one in which the pair have become closer and more at ease with each other, they moved it to a later slot in the schedule, allowing Portman and Christensen—strangers prior to the start of filming—more time to become acquainted. Ultimately, the dinner scene was shot a little more than three weeks into the production schedule, on

a stage set that featured faux marble walls, graceful columns, archways, and lush greenery.

During dinner, Anakin amuses Padmé by using his Jedi abilities to lift fruit from her plate and make it float in midair. Because the floating fruit would be a digital image added later, Christensen and Portman had to imagine its presence and movement across the table as they performed the scene. "We felt pretty stupid biting into fruit that didn't exist," Portman said, laughing. "But still, it was a fun scene to shoot. I don't think George was entirely satisfied with the dialogue he had written for the scene, because he told us to improvise some of the dialogue—and of course it got inappropriate very quickly!" Jonathan Hales, on the set during the filming of this scene, also rewrote some of the dialogue, reworking lines on the spot.

Trisha Biggar dubbed the gown worn by Padmé for the dinner scene the "leather and lace" outfit. "It was a beautiful gown with a very tight corset and matching gloves," Portman said. "Overall, what was different about the costumes in Episode II from those in Episode I was that they were made to make me

(Clockwise from top left) **Lucas** discusses with Portman the floating food that ILM will add later; lake retreat interiors—unlike the exteriors—were shot on stage sets built in Sydney; interior settings included a dining room and an intimate, fire-lit alcove—Trisha Biggar nicknamed Portman's elegant costume for the scene the "leather and lace" outfit.

look more like a woman. There were a lot of midriff-baring things and tight corsets. All of the costumes were very beautiful, and it was incredible to see the amount of work that went into them. It made me appreciate costumes in film so much more."

One of the most intensely romantic scenes at the retreat finds Anakin and Padmé sitting together in an inti-mate alcove, in front of a fire. There, in the firelight, they talk about their growing feelings for each other and the seeming impossibility of their sharing a life together. The scene typified the script's old-fashioned style. "Let's face it," Lucas admitted, "their dialogue in that scene is pretty corny. It is presented very honestly, it isn't tongue-in-cheek at all, and it's really played to the hilt. But it is consistent not only with the rest of this movie, but with the overall *Star Wars* style. Most people don't understand the style of *Star Wars*. They don't get that there is an underlying motif that is very much like a nineteen thirties western or Saturday matinee serial. It's in that more romantic period of making movies and adventure films. And this film is even more of a melodrama than the others."

That melodramatic style placed an additional acting burden on Hayden Christensen and Natalie Portman, who had to convey sincerity at the core of the stylized dialogue. "When I first read the script," Christensen commented, "a lot of the dialogue felt contrived and forced, and I was like,

'Oh, there's no way *that's* going to work.' But there is a way of speaking in the *Star Wars* universe, and it is acceptable because it is another galaxy, far, far away. Even though the themes are relevant to today, some of the dialogue is not—it's not supposed to be."

Anakin and Padmé share a lighter moment as they picnic in a meadow at the summer retreat. The establishing view of the picnic scene, also filmed at Lake Como, was the first visual-effects shot to be com-pleted for the movie, finaled by Pablo Helman in January 2001—three and a half months after the end of principal photography and *seventeen months* before the film's release. "It was a simple split shot," John Knoll recalled. "We had a plate from Como, with Padmé and Anakin sitting in the field, having their picnic. We added matte paintings to the background and CG shaaks—large, cowlike creatures—grazing nearby. A couple of shots of the two of them sitting there were in tight enough that there was no matte painting extension required; but even one of those required some effects work. George asked us to split Anakin out of one take and put him in the foreground of another. Pablo composited that shot himself, and it was our first final—only nineteen hundred and ninety-nine to go."

In a scene reminiscent of Paul Newman's bicycle sequence in *Butch Cassidy and the Sundance Kid*, Anakin

(Clockwise from left-hand page) For a lighthearted picnic scene at the lake retreat, live-action footage captured at Lake Como was enhanced by ILM with matte painted backgrounds and computer-generated, bovine shaaks; behind the scenes on the meadow; a publicity shot of Padmé; Christensen astride a blue-covered gimbal that will eventually be transformed into a digital shaak.

shows off for a laughing Padmé, performing stunts atop a shaak. While backgrounds and other live-action elements were captured at Lake Como, Hayden Christensen executed the riding stunts on stage in Australia, riding a shaak form mounted to a moving gimbal. Both the gimbal and the form were covered in blue material, later replaced with ILM's computer-generated animal. Fortunately for Christensen, the shaak was conceived as a slow-moving animal, and so the actions of the gimbal were fairly tame—a gentle, rocking movement. Even so, Christensen and Portman fell off the device during filming

of a final scene (subsequently cut from the film) in which Anakin and Padmé return to the retreat lodge, both astride the animal.

"Natalie was situated on the gimbal so that both of her legs were off to one side," Christensen recalled, "and when she started to go, she grabbed on to me and we both fell off. Nick Gillard and everybody else rushed to catch Natalie—'Natalie, Natalie, are you okay?' I was like, 'Hey, yeah, *I'm* okay, too.' But that was all right. We just hopped back on. It was a lot of fun to ride this thing. I'd see the people off to the side working the little crane for the gimbal, and I'd say, 'You're

not going to throw me off this time.' And they'd say, 'Oh, yes we are.' So there was kind of a competition going on between us."

Anakin's continuing nightmares about his mother mar the young lovers' idyllic experience at the summer retreat. As the nightmares intensify, Anakin makes the decision to return to Tatooine to find her. "She visits him in his dreams," Christensen said. "He sees her almost as an apparition; he knows that she is in pain and that he has to save her. That's what sends him on his journey. He is disobeying his mandate to protect Padmé, but she goes with him because of the love between them."

The pair board a Naboo starship for the trip to Tatooine. The construction department built the timber and fiberglass exterior of the craft for stationary live-action shots, while Peter Wyborn's model shop crew built the interior. In fact, the Naboo craft interior was the model shop's first assignment for the film. "It was also our biggest job," Wyborn noted. "We built all the control panels, creating a selection of buttons for the controls—if anyone had a spare hour or two, they'd be off making buttons. Then we molded them and cast them out of acrylic. We also made the chairs, which moved on tracks, as well as the steering column, console, and illuminated displays. That was quite a busy set, overall."

Determined to find the mother he hasn't seen since childhood, Anakin, with Padmé beside him, leaves the tranquillity and beauty of Naboo, plotting coordinates for Tatooine.

chapter
five

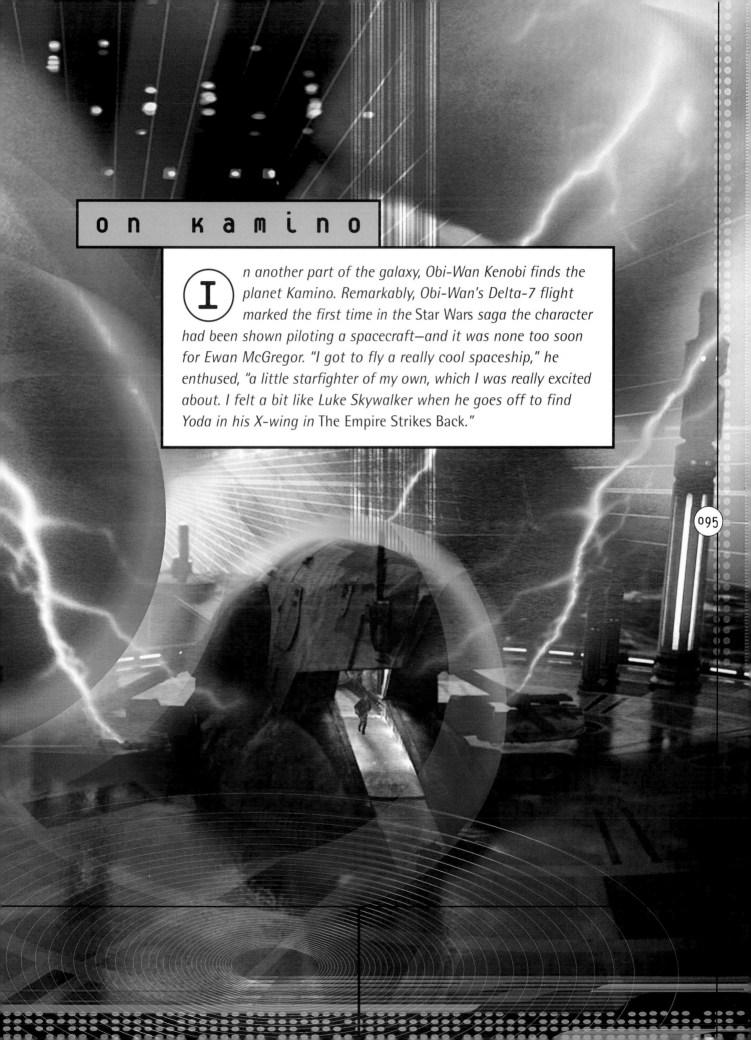

on kamino

I n another part of the galaxy, Obi-Wan Kenobi finds the planet Kamino. Remarkably, Obi-Wan's Delta-7 flight marked the first time in the Star Wars saga the character had been shown piloting a spacecraft—and it was none too soon for Ewan McGregor. "I got to fly a really cool spaceship," he enthused, "a little starfighter of my own, which I was really excited about. I felt a bit like Luke Skywalker when he goes off to find Yoda in his X-wing in The Empire Strikes Back."

The landing platform on Kamino required that a partial platform set be built on stage. Special effects supervisor Dave Young rigged an elaborate sprinkler system in the ceiling of the stage to produce continuous, controllable rainfall, and enormous fans produced wind on cue.

(R)ain and wind buffet the landing platform at Tipoca City, Kamino's capital, as Obi-Wan disembarks from his starship. A city of lights, Tipoca rests on giant stilts rising out of an ocean that covers the entire planet. Establishing views of the planet from space, and the rolling oceans were digital elements, while Tipoca City was a miniature. A section of the landing platform was built as a physical set on a stage in Sydney to accommodate a fight scene there between Obi-Wan and Jango Fett. The platform also provided a space on which to create a live rainstorm, alleviating the need to add digital rain effects to the live-action plates.

Lucas arrived on stage to shoot the Kamino platform a day ahead of schedule, and found the crews still finishing the set. "When George and the crew walked onto that set," Gavin Bocquet recalled, "the paint was still wet! It was on such a large stage—Stage One—we couldn't put giant heaters in there to get the paint to dry more quickly. All we could

(Inset, opposite)
For wide establishing shots of the platform rising from the stormy ocean on stilts, ILM built and shot a miniature, then composited that model photography with a computer-generated ocean. (Below) Final images were based on paintings by Erik Tiemens and (bottom) animatics by pre-visualization/effects supervisor Dan Gregoire.

Attack of the Clones marked the first time in the *Star Wars* saga that Obi-Wan Kenobi would be seen piloting a spacecraft —in this case, a Jedi starfighter Delta-7—as seen here in the rendering by Jay Shuster (right) and in the model (below, opposite) by John Duncan and painted by R. Kim Smith.

do was wait. We were always finishing a set as first unit came in to film it, but that was the closest call."

To create the rainstorm, Dave Young's special-effects department installed a ceiling-mounted rain system that covered the entire platform. "It had to be completely controllable," Young said, "so we could have rain wherever we were filming on the set. The rain would have to be switched off in the areas where the cameras were, but switched on in the areas of the actual action. The entire system was on solenoid valves, and we pumped in seven and a half tons of water per minute, covering an area of about a third of an acre. We used special rain heads that would throw out a square pattern and various-sized droplets, from large to mist-sized, so we could alter the size of the droplets *and* the size of the spread, as needed."

Ridding the stage of the enormous amounts of water was the most difficult part of the setup. "We had to completely seal the stage," Young explained, "then redirect the water out the doors. On top of the rain, there was a lot of wind. Since there was a shortage of wind machines in Sydney, we wound up building one from scratch in only four days."

Lucas's watery vision of Kamino stemmed from the logic that, because the sea is the cradle of all biological evolution, cloners might choose to base their operation on an ocean planet. "They are re-creating life there," Lucas commented, "and Kaminoans are creatures that began life in the sea—they might have been something like dolphins or salamanders at one point. Then they got arms and larger brains, and they began moving out of the water and building these technological cities. They are now a very advanced technological culture."

In Tipoca City, Obi-Wan is cordially greeted by Kamino native Taun We, voiced by Rena Owen. All of the Kaminoans were computer-generated characters, modeled in the months after the shoot by Geoff Campbell and his team at ILM, based on designs conceived in the Ranch art department. Their design was atypical of previous *Star Wars* characters in that they resembled the classic alien Steven Spielberg had committed to film in *Close Encounters of the Third Kind*—tall, graceful, benevolent creatures with very large, dark, almond-shaped eyes and underdeveloped mouths and noses.

"The Kamino design was a very deliberate nod to the classic alien of *Close Encounters*," Lucas admitted. "Steven had done a lot of research on that film and really drew

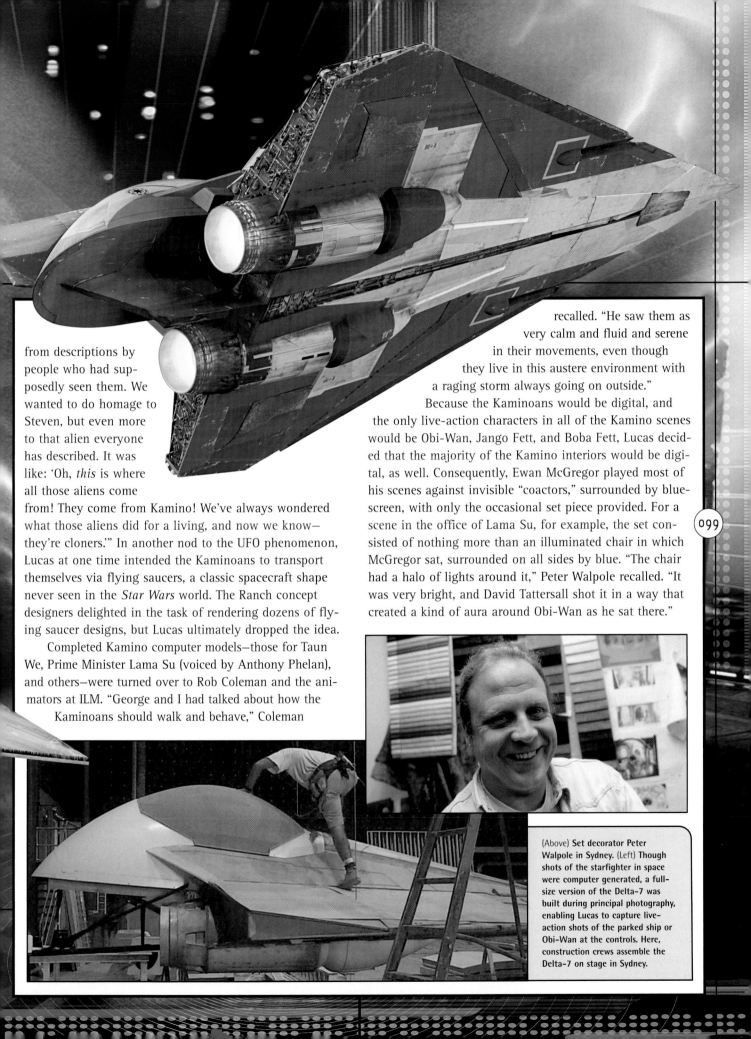

from descriptions by people who had supposedly seen them. We wanted to do homage to Steven, but even more to that alien everyone has described. It was like: 'Oh, *this* is where all those aliens come from! They come from Kamino! We've always wondered what those aliens did for a living, and now we know—they're cloners.'" In another nod to the UFO phenomenon, Lucas at one time intended the Kaminoans to transport themselves via flying saucers, a classic spacecraft shape never seen in the *Star Wars* world. The Ranch concept designers delighted in the task of rendering dozens of flying saucer designs, but Lucas ultimately dropped the idea.

Completed Kamino computer models—those for Taun We, Prime Minister Lama Su (voiced by Anthony Phelan), and others—were turned over to Rob Coleman and the animators at ILM. "George and I had talked about how the Kaminoans should walk and behave," Coleman

recalled. "He saw them as very calm and fluid and serene in their movements, even though they live in this austere environment with a raging storm always going on outside."

Because the Kaminoans would be digital, and the only live-action characters in all of the Kamino scenes would be Obi-Wan, Jango Fett, and Boba Fett, Lucas decided that the majority of the Kamino interiors would be digital, as well. Consequently, Ewan McGregor played most of his scenes against invisible "coactors," surrounded by bluescreen, with only the occasional set piece provided. For a scene in the office of Lama Su, for example, the set consisted of nothing more than an illuminated chair in which McGregor sat, surrounded on all sides by blue. "The chair had a halo of lights around it," Peter Walpole recalled. "It was very bright, and David Tattersall shot it in a way that created a kind of aura around Obi-Wan as he sat there."

(Above) Set decorator Peter Walpole in Sydney. (Left) Though shots of the starfighter in space were computer generated, a full-size version of the Delta-7 was built during principal photography, enabling Lucas to capture live-action shots of the parked ship or Obi-Wan at the controls. Here, construction crews assemble the Delta-7 on stage in Sydney.

(Left) The design for the Kaminoans was closer to the traditional extraterrestrial concept than any alien ever featured in *Star Wars*, as shown here in this model by concept sculptor Robert E. Barnes. (Above and below) Because the Kaminoans were considerably taller than humans, voice actor Anthony Phelan (Lama Su) wore a hard hat to which a head cutout had been attached to ensure proper eye contact with other actors.

From Lama Su, Obi-Wan learns that a Jedi Master named Sifo-Dyas had commissioned the Kaminoans to build a massive army of clones for the Republic ten years before. Obi-Wan is then given a tour of the cloning facilities, a series of all-bluescreen shots for which McGregor didn't even have a chair to ground him. "The big walk-through scenes were more or less just Ewan walking across a floor that would be added to later, digitally," Gavin Bocquet noted. "The floor was mirrored so that ILM would have reflections to put into the digital, highly polished white and black floors that would eventually be there. They spent one whole morning just shooting Ewan walking these blue corridors—looking amazed in one shot, in awe in another,

just as reactions to what the Kaminoans were showing him. But there was nothing there! It must have been very difficult for Ewan."

"Nobody really understood what was going on," John Knoll added, "except George. George would say, 'Okay, over to your left you're seeing all the cloning chambers,' and Ewan would walk along and react to those cues. He had nothing else to go on. There was nothing but blue floor, blue walls, blue everywhere."

In the course of his tour, Obi-Wan is shown classrooms filled with school-aged clones, a commissary where twenty-year-old clones eat, and,

(Left) A crew member stands next to cardboard cutouts of the Kaminoans and the suited-up Boba Fett to illustrate the size disparity between the human characters and the aliens. (Right) A sculpt of a Kaminoan by Michael Murnane.

(Above) Obi-Wan is greeted by Taun We (voiced by Rena Owen) on the Kamino landing platform. (Below) In a meeting with Kamino prime minister Lama Su (voiced by Anthony Phelan), Obi-Wan learns that a mysterious Jedi Master ordered the creation of a clone army ten years before.

the fully developed clones. All helmeted and armored clones were computer generated at ILM.

News from Obi-Wan regarding the clone army prompts greater dissension between members of the Galactic Senate and eventually leads to their bestowing upon Chancellor Palpatine emergency executive powers—powers the Chancellor "reluctantly" accepts.

When Lucas first began contriving the backstory for the Star Wars saga in the mid-1970s, newspaper headlines were full of the Watergate scandal, a real-life event that influenced the young writer-director as he crafted the political chaos of his cinematic fantasy. "The political issues have to do

from a balcony, a parade ground featuring thousands of grown, armored clone troopers—all created from the DNA of bounty hunter Jango Fett. ILM did its own bit of cloning for the sequence, digitally replicating shots of thirteen-year-old Daniel Logan for the young, school-aged clones, Bodie Taylor for the twenty-year-old versions, and Temuera Morrison for

For a sequence in which Obi-Wan is given a tour of the cloning facilities, Ewan McGregor walked a blue-screen stage alone, without coactors, sets, or props with which to interact. Miniatures provided the corridors. Rooms seen through the corridor glass panels—such as the hatchery—were computer-generated sets.

with democracies that give their countries over to a dictator because of a crisis of some kind," Lucas stated, "about people who live in a democracy and then *willingly* give it up, allowing whoever is in office to stay there. This was a very big issue when I was writing the first *Star Wars* because it was soon after Nixon's presidency, and there was a point, right before he was thrown out of office, where he suggested that they change a constitutional amendment so that he could run for a third term. Even when he started getting into trouble, he was saying, 'If the military will back me, I'll stay in office.' His idea was: 'To hell with Congress and potential impeachment. I'll go directly to the army, and between the army and myself, I'll continue to be president.' That is what happens here. An emergency in the Republic leads the Senate to make Palpatine, essentially, 'dictator for life.' And now, with the clones, he has an army."

A temporary composite of a scene from the tour sequence features the McGregor blue-screen element, roughed-in CG Kamino characters, and a sketch of the armory below.

(A)fter the tour of the cloning operation, Obi-Wan is taken by Taun We to meet Jango Fett in his Kamino apartment. When they arrive, the door is answered by Jango's ten-year-old cloned son, Boba Fett. Shot in the last week of July 2000, the scene was the first of the production for actors Daniel Logan and Temuera Morrison, both natives of New Zealand. Morrison had been cast based on his riveting lead performance in *Once Were Warriors*, a 1994 domestic drama from New Zealand, directed by Lee Tamahori.

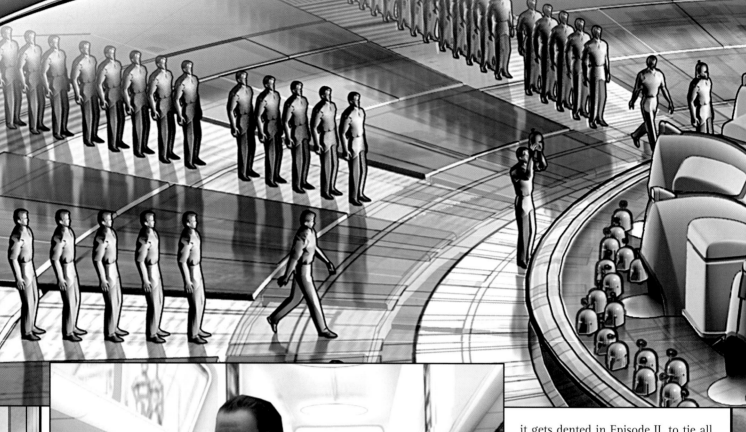

Animatics troopers at training consoles. Views of the armored and helmeted clones were all computer generated.

On the set Logan appeared unfazed by his *Star Wars* stint, but Morrison's first day, in particular, was a nerve-wracking one for him. "That first day was a bit intimidating," he recalled, "just because of the scale of *Star Wars* and the numbers of people involved. But George said to me: 'Hey, you can relax. This is just another day at the office. No big deal.'"

Because Jango Fett is the predecessor to the adult Boba Fett character *and* the stormtroopers established in the original *Star Wars*, Morrison's costume featured elements of both designs. "I wanted Jango's outfit to be very close to what Boba wears in the later films," Lucas said, "as if Boba just takes that outfit over and modifies it to his own taste. But I also wanted the outfit to be reminiscent of what a stormtrooper looked like, so we made a simpler, cleaner version of the Boba Fett costume."

Costume features that served to connect Jango with Boba Fett included a dark blue undersuit and a helmet that was a copy of the original Boba Fett headpiece. "There is a dent in that helmet in Episode IV," Trisha Biggar noted, "and

it gets dented in Episode II, to tie all of that in. Then, to suggest the stormtrooper, Jango Fett's costume was originally going to be white. We were trying out some new material for the armor, and we got to a stage where it was a fantastic silver color. I thought we should let George see that before we went any further. He really liked it, and decided we should leave it this burnished-steel color."

"The white didn't fit this movie in terms of who and what Jango Fett was," Lucas added. "It looked too slick. I needed something a little rougher than that, but still reminiscent of the stormtroopers, so that the audience would get the connection between them and Jango Fett." Jango's burnished-metal-looking armor was made of fiberglass to which aluminum powder had been added. To avoid injuries, stunt versions of the armor were made out of a softer, injected-foam material, worn by stuntmen during fight sequences. Seven sets of Jango armor were built—four hero versions for close-ups, and three for stunt work. Each set consisted of 25 separate pieces, a total of 175 costume prop pieces for Jango alone.

Jango Fett's apartment, like all of the Kamino interiors, had a high-tech, polished look that was stylistically in keeping with his costume. "With Jango Fett's apartment," Peter Walpole stated, "we felt that we were presenting a bit of history. There is a huge Boba Fett following, especially in the States, and here we had his dad living on Kamino. The set was very white, stark, and

Clone troopers amass for training in an ILM computer-enhanced rendering (left) and in the final shot (right). Three actors portrayed the clones—derived from the DNA of Jango Fett—at different stages of maturity.

stylized. It also had a lot of black Plexiglas in the walls and floors. We built a black settee, which was molded into the set, and a couple of other furniture pieces. The Kaminoans are eight feet tall, so most of the tables and chairs, in proportion to a normal human being, would be slightly higher. But we didn't want to make it look like something from the *Land of the Giants*, so it was a subtle thing. When adults sat in these chairs, their legs wouldn't quite reach the ground. We reasoned that Jango Fett wouldn't have changed the furniture there to fit him better. He was just living within the Kaminoans' environment."

Ordered by the Jedi Council to bring Jango back to Coruscant for questioning, Obi-Wan confronts the escaping bounty hunter on the rain-drenched landing platform, where one of the film's major fight sequences was set. Lucas, Nick Gillard, the actors, and stunt people all relied on animatics to tell them what action they needed to capture and from what camera angles. David Dozoretz and his team had included in the animatics three-dimensional models of Jango and Obi-Wan, animated via motion capture, a technology through which the actions of a real person—outfitted in a suit dotted with special markers—are "captured" in the computer, providing a basis for computer animation.

"We went to ILM," Dozoretz recalled, "and worked with Jeff Light, who is the motion capture supervisor there. We

For a mess-hall scene, ILM shot actor Bodie Taylor—who portrayed the Jango clone at age 20—multiple times and in various positions. ILM then digitally "cloned" the footage, replicating the shots to fill the mess hall set with hundreds of dining troopers.

Jango Fett (standing) is the predecessor to his cloned son, Boba Fett (top, as seen in *A New Hope*) and his multiple genetic offspring—predecessors to the stormtroopers introduced in the original *Star Wars* (middle). Fully armored CG clones in Episode II were animated through motion-capture, a technique in which a performer in a special suit executes actions that are "captured" in the computer.

august 7, 2000
fox studios, sydney

Halfway through the shoot, the crew prepares to film Dex's Diner, where Obi-Wan visits old friend Dexter Jettster to inquire about a toxic dart he has extracted from the neck of assassin Zam Wesell.

A technician walks onto the set—which was inspired by diners of the 1950s and '60s—smiles, and says, "Looks just like *American Graffiti!*" Intermingled with chrome and red vinyl set pieces are bizarre-looking, yet vaguely

The "big food" on the menu at Dexter's Diner. Prop personnel searched for bizarre-looking roots and other exotic pieces of produce to create an alien-looking buffet.

familiar foodstuffs. There are meringue pastries, but the meringue is a vivid blue. There are Rice Krispie Treat–like bars, but they are grossly oversized. In fact, *big food* seems to be a specialty at Dex's Diner. Giant, multi-decker sandwiches made up of lettuce, pineapple, cheese, and extra-large slabs of processed ham and chicken on massive rolls are laid out artfully on trays.

Extras dressed in elaborate costumes file into the diner, some taking seats at the counter, others at booths. George Lucas surveys the set, looks over the placement of food on the counter, and slightly repositions a platter of über-pastries. Meanwhile, Ewan McGregor, in Jedi garb, and Ron Falk—who will be the voice of the computer-animated Dex—talk at one of the empty booths. Lucas shows the actors a maquette of Dexter, giving McGregor a sense of whom he will be talking to and Falk a sense of whom he will be portraying.

Animation director Rob Coleman is also on the set, conferring with Lucas regarding the computer-generated Dex. Lucas recalls a montage of eyes he saw at the opening of a television show, and asks Coleman to find that piece of footage. "These eyes are Watto's eyes," he says, referring to the Dexter concept illustration. "Let's see if we can come up with something different."

"Do you want to play him the same size as the actor?" Coleman asks, eyeing Falk's large frame.

"Yeah."

"So he doesn't quite fit in the booth when he sits down to talk to Obi-Wan?"

"Yeah..." Lucas smiles.

All is ready for a rehearsal. The physical-effects crew cues machines situated in the kitchen area, and steam begins to rise from behind the counter. Obi-Wan Kenobi enters the diner and asks to see Dexter Jettster. An actress playing a waitress—who will be replaced with a droid server—calls out, "Someone to see you, honey," toward the kitchen. "A Jedi, by the looks of him." The waitress then

The world-wise Dexter Jettster (voiced by Ronald Falk)—now proprietor of Dexter's Diner—appears at an order window.

offers Obi-Wan a cup of "Jawa juice."

Falk-as-Dexter ambles out of the kitchen to greet Obi-Wan. The actors get to the end of the scripted scene—but with Lucas preoccupied, no one says, "Cut." There is an awkward pause; and then McGregor looks around and says, "I love what you've done with the place."

"Cut!"

107

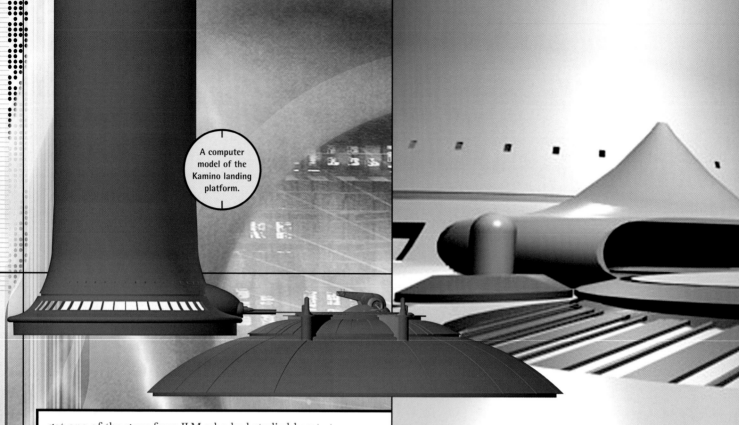

A computer model of the Kamino landing platform.

got one of the guys from ILM who had studied karate to come over, and we had him do a lot of hand-to-hand combat movements—flips and all kinds of things. There had been a very quick storyboarding process for the fight right before George left for Australia; we emulated those storyboards in the animatics, and came up with some of our own action, as well. We transferred the animatics over to Australia by way of a private virtual network, so George could see what we were doing and comment on it. We managed to do something like a

hundred shots in a week and a half so they would have the animatics in time to use them on set."

The landing platform clash between Obi-Wan and Jango Fett was Ewan McGregor's most complex fight scene in the movie, worked out in a number of choreography sessions with Nick Gillard. "I did one day of the fight scene in the rain," Temuera Morrison recalled, "and that was enough. The helmet was a bit claustrophobic, and it made breathing a bit of a problem. I'd breathe, and it would fog up and I couldn't see anything. I also couldn't hear anything inside it, so I'd be standing there, wondering if they'd said 'action' or not. I was very glad they were able to find a good-looking stunt double who could match me and do most of the fight scene in the rain. When he showed up, I said: 'Here, mate, here's my helmet. *You* stick this on and go get wet for two days!'"

While Lucas shot close-ups and other pieces of the Obi–Jango fight with McGregor and Morrison, Ben Burtt shot their stunt doubles in second unit. Unlike *The Phantom Menace*, *Attack of the Clones* didn't have a dedicated second-unit crew working separately from the main unit.

The computer-generated Taun We was added to the live-action plate in postproduction.

108

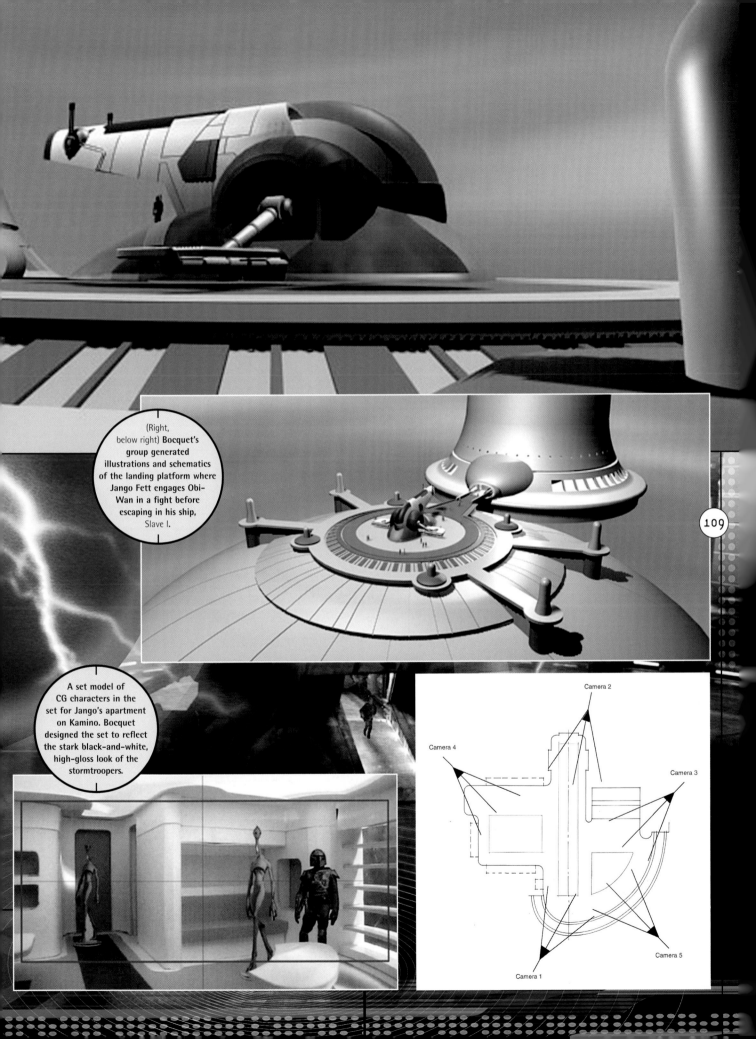

(Right, below right) **Bocquet's** group generated illustrations and schematics of the landing platform where Jango Fett engages Obi-Wan in a fight before escaping in his ship, Slave I.

A set model of CG characters in the set for Jango's apartment on Kamino. Bocquet designed the set to reflect the stark black-and-white, high-gloss look of the stormtroopers.

Camera 1

Camera 2

Camera 3

Camera 4

Camera 5

Rather, after a week or so of first-unit filming, a handful of second-unit shots would accumulate; then, in a single day, Burtt and a very small camera crew would capture those shots. "In essence," Burtt said, "second unit functioned as an ad hoc group that formed for a day, then broke apart until it was needed again."

In part, the second-unit burden for Episode II was uncharacteristically light due to Lucas's intention to capture more difficult stunts with computer-generated replicas of the actors created at ILM. "We used a lot more digital stuntmen in Episode II than we've ever used before," Lucas said. "They had to look as real as the actor, which had been a challenge before, but this time I think we licked it. In some of the stunts and more elaborate sequences, you won't know if you're looking at the real actor or a digital reproduction. We were able to create an identical clone, a much more accurate representation of the actor than what we often get with a stunt double."

Because the digital stuntmen would be featured so prominently in the film, their research and development had been a major area of concern for the crews at ILM. "We rose to a whole new level of realism with the digital stuntmen," John Knoll said. "Our mandate

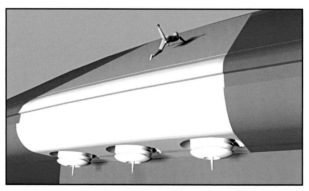

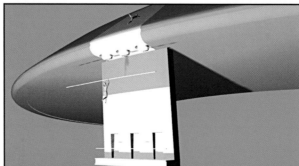

from George was that the digital stunt doubles had to work from about the knees up, which meant much more realistic clothing, hair, and skin than we'd ever done before." As a start, all the principal actors were cyberscanned, not only to aid the digital stunt double assignment but also to ensure accuracy in the toy action figures that would be marketed and sold with the movie's release. The cyberscanning process involved aiming a laser light and camera at a subject—in this case, the actors—positioned on a 360-degree turntable. Revolving around the subject, the laser picked up a contoured image that was recorded by the camera and could be transferred as a computer file to form the basis of the computer model. Typically, a full head scan took approximately seventeen seconds to complete.

Despite the liberal use of digital stuntmen for the Obi-Jango fight scene, the tightness of the schedule and the complexity of the fight made it impossible for Lucas and the second unit to shoot it in its entirety during principal

The entire Jango-Obi-Wan combat sequence was first worked out in animatics. From those, Lucas determined how much of the battle he could shoot live on a set and how much would have to be created digitally by ILM.

Obi-Wan and Jango Fett fight on the rain-drenched landing platform. Lucas shot McGregor and Morrison or their stunt doubles for two days in Sydney, then picked up additional shots in London after the end of principal photography. The sequence also featured digital stuntmen, which enabled Lucas to realize dynamic, acrobatic fight moves without resorting to cumbersome wire harnesses or other stunt rigs.

As he had for *The Phantom Menace*, **Nick** Gillard choreographed all the film's fight sequences, spending weeks and months training the principals in martial arts and fencing techniques. Gillard approached each fight as a story in its own right, with a beginning, middle, and end, writing out fight vignettes that were then translated into stationary story-boards (as shown below, by story-board artist Mark Sexton) or moving animatics.

OBI-WAN & JANGO FETT FIGHT   PAGE 9

32.

OBI-WAN LANDS ON HIS FEET

33.

JANGO QUICKLY RECOVERS AND ATTACKS

34a.

34b.

OBI-WAN BLOCKS JANGO AS HE SWINGS HIS GUN UP TO FIRE....
AND THE PAIR STRUGGLE FOR THE WEAPON

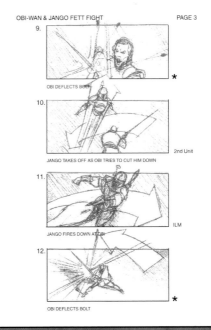

OBI-WAN & JANGO FETT FIGHT   PAGE 3

9.

OBI DEFLECTS BOLT

10.   2nd Unit

JANGO TAKES OFF AS OBI TRIES TO CUT HIM DOWN

11.   ILM

JANGO FIRES DOWN AT OBI

12.

OBI DEFLECTS BOLT

113

photography. Remaining shots were captured in March 2001, during the first of the two pickup shoots at Ealing Studios.

Jango ultimately gets the upper hand in the fight, and he and his son escape Kamino in Jango's *Slave I,* soon followed by Obi-Wan in his Delta-7. As both ships near the planet of Geonosis, they engage in a chase through an asteroid field. As in the earlier airspeeder chase, computer-generated backgrounds and ships were intercut with live-action shots of McGregor and Morrison in their respective cockpits. Though a few slight banking shots were captured by mounting the ships to Dave Young's gimbal, most of the dynamic action was simulated by camera moves, because these ships—unlike the speeders—were too large for the gimbal to handle easily. Camera shake and other effects were added by ILM in the compositing stage, to add excitement to the shots.

As before, animatics projected on large plasma screens guided the actors as they performed within the cockpit sets. "It was amazing," Morrison recalled. "When we showed up on the set, they had already made an animated version of the scene we were about to shoot. They were able to put that up on the screen and we'd see it there—the whole chase sequence already cut together. It would cut to an interior of the spaceship, so I could see where I was in the scene and create the appropriate action. It was nice to see the animated bits, so we could get a clear idea of what they were after."

Obi-Wan maneuvers his starfighter through the asteroid belt, and shadows Jango Fett's

Obi-Wan—whom Jango believes has died in a fall over the side of the platform—prepares to throw a tracing beacon onto the side of the departing Slave I.

Slave I to land on the redrock planet of Geonosis, uncertain as to what awaits him there.

114

Slave I—originally
introduced as Boba Fett's
ship in The Empire Strikes Back—was
a computer-generated construct
throughout, with only the cockpit built
live and in full-scale for shots of Boba
and Jango at the controls. Because the
original Slave I model was on exhibit at
the Smithsonian, the computer modelers
at ILM relied on photographic
reference from the earlier film
to realize the craft.

In a scene reminiscent of the asteroid-field dogfight in The Empire Strikes Back (top), Obi-Wan tracks Jango Fett through an asteroid belt. Technological innovations made since Empire meant this chase would feature greater freedom of movement and more spectacular visual and audio effects.

To create a satisfying audio effect for the seismic explosion, sound designer Ben Burtt inserted an ominous moment of silence that serves to both delineate it from the noise of the asteroid pursuit and to anticipate the weapon's deadly burst. Originally, the pursuit was designed as a slower game of submarinelike cat-and-mouse, with Jango dropping the seismic weapons from above—as if they were depth charges—on an unsuspecting Obi-Wan. After the first cut, the concept was discarded in favor of a speedier chase for reasons of pacing.

chapter
six

on tatooine

As Obi-Wan explores Geonosis, Padmé and Anakin arrive in Mos Espa, visiting the junk trader—and Anakin's former owner—Watto (voiced by Andy Secombe) to learn the whereabouts of Shmi Skywalker.

T he day-and-a-half shoot for the Mos Espa scenes, scheduled for the second week of September 2000, marked a return for many members of the cast and crew to Tozeur, Tunisia, where Mos Espa had been built originally for *The Phantom Menace*. The move there was extremely labor-intensive, requiring the transportation of hundreds of costumes, creature masks, makeup supplies, and construction materials and tools.

Situated on the sand dunes just outside the town, the set had been maintained continuously in the three years since the Episode I shoot, both because Rick McCallum knew that production would most likely be returning there for Episode II and because Mos Espa had become a tourist attraction in its own right.

"Tozeur is on the tourist route," Gavin Bocquet commented, "and so the Tunisian Tourist Board was interested in maintaining the *Star Wars* set as an added attraction for the tourists. In fact, they actually added a bit to the Mos Espa set. We'd finished off only the parts of the buildings that the camera would see, but they finished off more of the buildings, and added others."

When production returned to the site for Episode II, they found the town remarkably intact.

(Above) On Tatooine, Anakin and Padmé visit junk dealer Watto (voiced by Andrew Secombe) to learn the whereabouts of Shmi Skywalker. (Below) On location in Tunisia, where all the Tatooine sequences were shot, George Lucas directs a C-3PO–suited Anthony Daniels.

"It looked pretty good," Bocquet said, "especially considering that some of it had blown down in a mad sandstorm when we were there the first time. Fortunately, they hadn't had a storm as bad as that in the three years since. The only thing that had gone was the paint. It's very windy and there is a lot of sand, creating a sandblasting effect that had taken the paint all the way back to the plaster; so we had to refurbish about two-thirds of the main street."

Peter Walpole and the Tunisian crews were tasked with re-creating the look of the town established in the last film, but unfortunately none of the props or set dressings from *The Phantom Menace* had survived. "They hadn't stored them because they only archive the most important stuff, and these dressings were all very scrap-oriented," Walpole explained. "So we re-created the market stalls. The Tunisian prop master, Mohamed Bargaoui, was the same as last time, so there was continuity there; and he had very talented craftsmen who made

The chrome, dart-shaped Naboo starship in which Padmé and Anakin travel to Tatooine was computer-modeled to resemble the original ship from Episode I.

The *Attack of the Clones* production crew returned to the Tunisian troglodyte dwellings that had served as a homestead location for the original *Star Wars* (above). Many of the stairways and other structural details added to the site for the first film were still intact after nearly a quarter-century (below).

(Right and far right)
Luke with Owen and Beru in A New Hope; Anakin and Padmé with Cliegg Lars and—a younger—Owen and Beru in Attack of the Clones. Upon his arrival in Tunisia, Lucas was dismayed because he thought that the ceiling pattern, originally created by production designer John Barry in 1976, was different from what he remembered, and he assumed that someone had altered it in the years since Star Wars. A look at stills from the original film assured the director that the pattern had remained unchanged.

all the props for the market stalls and streets." Other Tunisian crew members returning to the *Star Wars* fold were art director Taieb Jallouli and production supervisor Abdelaziz Ben Mlouka. "Those people are all part of the family," Rick McCallum commented.

Production filmed the scene at Watto's shop in a single day at the Tozeur location, along with shots of Anakin and Padmé being transported through the town by a droid-driven rickshaw. A truck actually towed the rickshaw, with

Lucas had used two locations in Tunisia to create the homestead from which a restless and rebellious teenager named Luke Skywalker yearned to escape. Interiors such as the kitchen–dining area had been shot near the town of Matmata, within sunken, cavelike dwellings carved into the desert by the area's troglodyte peoples hundreds of years ago, and since converted into a hotel. The farm's topside, igloo-style buildings had been filmed on a nearby salt flat called the Chott el Jerid.

(Left) Other homestead scenes were shot at the Chott el Jerid, in the precise spot the original homestead exteriors had been filmed. (Right) Lucas in Tunisia with first assistant director James McTeigue.

Portman and Christensen inside, through the set. In postproduction, ILM painted out the truck and replaced it with the computer-generated droid.

F rom Watto, Anakin and Padmé learn that a moisture farmer named Cliegg Lars had fallen in love with Shmi—then had bought her in order to free her and, later, marry her. With this knowledge, they leave for the Lars homestead near the town of Mos Eisley, a remote area of Tatooine. Twenty-five years earlier, George

The same approach was taken for the latest episode. When the *Attack of the Clones* crew arrived on the salt flat early in September 2000, they saw little evidence of the first production's presence there two decades before. The original sets had been buried under twenty-five years' worth of desert sand drifts, so crew members had to completely rebuild the igloo structures. What did remain was a slight

impression in the ground, marking the three-foot-tall rim of a room-sized crater that had been excavated for the *Star Wars* shoot.

"It was amazing that even that was still there!" Bocquet remarked. "But we were fortunate that it was, because otherwise finding the exact same spot would have been like finding a needle in a haystack. The set could have been put up somewhere else on the flat, and it would have looked fine—but there was something quite nice about being in the exact same place where the original film had been shot."

Bocquet's crew used archived technical drawings of the original homestead to re-create the set, but found that the drawings were often inaccurate. "We began to realize that whatever they had *planned* to do when they drew those drawings in London for the first film," Bocquet noted, "they must have changed their minds once they got to the site—because what they built and what was on the drawings were two very different things. Even the dressings had changed. There'd be something indicated in the drawings; but then, obviously, once they'd arrived at the location, they'd found other things to use—odd bits of junk—and they'd thrown that in on the spot. So we couldn't trust the drawings. We constantly had to double-check what had actually wound up in the first movie. It was wonderful, though, to try to re-create that set. The homestead was at the very heart of *Star Wars*."

Fortunately, production found the troglodyte dwellings near Matmata mostly unchanged; in fact, even some of the structural details that production designer John Barry had added for the original *Star Wars* shoot—door trims, decks, and stairways—were still there, along with a black-and-brown pattern Barry's crew had made in a ceiling for the

dining scene between Luke, Uncle Owen, and Aunt Beru. "That room was originally a kitchen," Bocquet recalled, "and the ceiling had become black from smoke. So John Barry had just scraped out some of that blackened area going back to the red mud of the cave, which had created a pattern—a rather primitive design that you could see above Luke's head in the ceiling. And that was still there after twenty-five years!"

Some refurbishing of the dwellings was required for *Attack of the Clones*, however. While slight alterations could be justified by the fact that the events of Episode II took place twenty years before those of Episode IV, overall the homestead had to be made to look exactly as it had in the first film. What made the task especially challenging was that the making of the first *Star Wars* had not been well documented in photographs or behind-the-scenes footage. "Who knew, when it was being made, that it was going to be so wildly successful?" Bocquet commented. "So there was virtually no reference on the making of the movie. We

august 25, 2000
fox studios, sydney

This is the last day of filming in Australia. It is a Friday. On Monday, the cast and crew will leave for Lake Como, Italy, the first leg of a nearly three-week-long location stint that will also take them to Tunisia and, briefly, to Spain.

It is late afternoon, and the crew has been shooting interiors of Padmé's childhood home in Theed since morning (a scene that will not make the final cut but which is included on the Episode II DVD). Now they are filming the last setup on the day's schedule in a beautiful salmon-colored kitchen, a small set cramped with actors, crew members, and camera and lighting equipment. Natalie Portman is sitting in a makeup chair, her hair hanging long and curly, dressed in a sea-green gown that reveals her back and midriff. She smiles as she rises from the chair, thanking the makeup artist who has just touched up her face.

On Lucas's cue, Portman—along with Claudia Karvan and Trisha Noble, who play her sister, Sola, and her mother, Jobal, respectively—begins a scene in which Padmé denies her feelings for Anakin and his for her. After shooting a first take, Portman and Lucas discuss the scene quietly. "It was very good," Lucas assures her, speaking of the last take. "Let's just do one more."

The crew sets up to do another one.

"Let's go again, please!" James McTeigue shouts out in his polite, cordial manner. The set instantly falls silent, cameras roll, and the scene is repeated.

In a scene cut from the final film, Anakin and Padmé visit her family at her childhood home in Theed. Gavin Bocquet and his crew had designed and built a beautiful, salmon-colored home interior set that included a kitchen and main dining area.

Lucas says, "Cut!" There is a palpable tension in the silence that follows, as everyone waits to hear his reaction to this take. If he is pleased, their work in Sydney is done. If he is not, the shooting day continues.

Lucas casually strolls out from behind his monitor toward the expectant, waiting crew. "Well," he says slowly, "offhand, I'd say we're on the wrong set, in the wrong city, on the wrong continent."

The crew applauds and whistles loudly. Even Lucas, normally reserved, whoops and claps. A smiling Portman gives him a hug.

"Thanks everybody," Lucas says to the crew. "See you at the party tonight."

The two-month shoot in Sydney is completed.

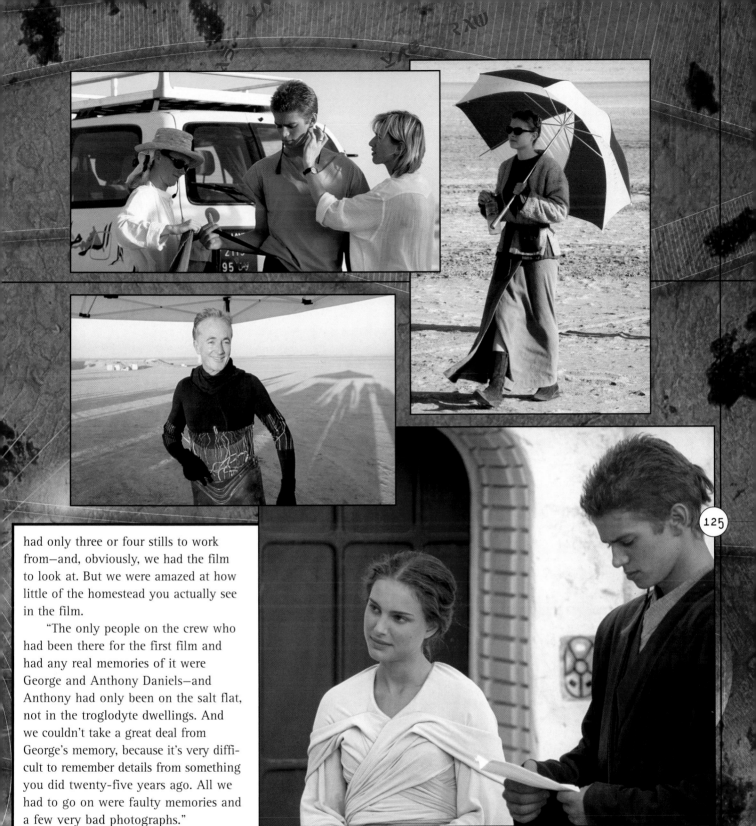

had only three or four stills to work from—and, obviously, we had the film to look at. But we were amazed at how little of the homestead you actually see in the film.

"The only people on the crew who had been there for the first film and had any real memories of it were George and Anthony Daniels—and Anthony had only been on the salt flat, not in the troglodyte dwellings. And we couldn't take a great deal from George's memory, because it's very difficult to remember details from something you did twenty-five years ago. All we had to go on were faulty memories and a few very bad photographs."

As evidence of the tricks memory can play, when Bocquet first showed photographs of the troglodyte dwelling dining area to Lucas, the director expressed dismay that the patterned ceiling had been changed. "He said, 'Oh, no—they've painted it and put a different pattern up there,'" Bocquet recalled. "He was the only one of us who had been there originally, so we had no reason to argue with him. Then we looked at refer-

(Clockwise from top left) Makeup artist Lynn Wheeler attends to Hayden Christensen on location in Tunisia; sixteen-year-old Sydney native Bonnie Piesse was cast as Beru Whitesun—future aunt to Luke Skywalker; Portman and Christensen wait between setups at the homestead location; Anthony Daniels, in a partial C-3PO suit, finds shelter from Tunisia's ubiquitous sunlight.

ence photographs from the first film, went back, and took photographs from the same position, and it showed that the ceiling pattern *was* the same. It's not that we wanted to prove him wrong; it is just the way the memory works."

By the time production arrived at the location, art department and construction crews had recaptured the original look of the dwellings. For George Lucas, more than anyone else on the crew, the return to the homestead site was a poignant occasion. "It was a very nostalgic experience," he admitted. "It was odd to be back in one of the places we shot the original movie, especially since it hadn't changed much. It was strange to be standing in the same spot twenty-five years later. It was the same thing I always felt whenever Harrison Ford showed up on the set in the Indiana Jones outfit: 'Here we are again.' In this case, we were going back to one of the real iconic locations of *Star Wars*. There we were, standing in the same place, doing the same thing.

"But there were differences. Last time I was there, I was under a lot of pressure. I didn't have any idea of where my life was going or where this movie was going. Last time, I was in a lot of trouble. This time, it was a much more mellow experience. I was just continuing the story and having fun."

The significance of the return to the site was not lost on the crew members, who quietly gathered round as Lucas stepped on the set for the first time. "Even when the crews walked onto those sets," Bocquet recalled, "there was a kind of quiet pause and contemplation. These environments were where you first met and got to know Luke Skywalker, See-Threepio, and Artoo-Detoo. Those things were very strong in people's memories." The excitement

among the crew members spread to the locals, many of whom gathered to watch the shoot, taking quick peeks beneath the giant silk David Tattersall had extended over the dwelling cavity as a means of softening and diffusing the harsh desert sunlight.

(Above, from left to right) Joel Edgerton, Australian assistant to Rick McCallum Jacqui Louez, McCallum, and Lucas on the Chott el Jerid. (Below) Natalie Portman enjoys a light moment on the garage set between takes.

The cast members—even those who had not yet been born when the original film was made—also experienced a sense of re-creating history. Australian actor Joel Edgerton, cast as the young Owen Lars, fell into that category, yet still felt an obligation to the characterizations established in *A New Hope*. "It was quite amazing to step into a role that already existed," Edgerton noted. "To be able to watch what another actor had done twenty-five years earlier with the same role was a bit bizarre—but it also provided a guide as to where I

126

Anakin confesses
his slaughter of the
Tusken Raider camp to Padmé
in the homestead garage. Like
many other sets in the homestead sequence, the garage
featured in the original Star
Wars had to be meticulously
re-created.

should pitch the character now, as a younger man. Phil Brown, who originally played the role of an older Owen Lars, portrayed him as quite straightforward and to the point; and he wasn't a very animated man. There was that choice to be made—would he have been more animated and energetic as a younger man? What does working a moisture farm for twenty-five years do to someone? Because he might have changed quite a bit in that length of time, I had license to play him pretty much how I wanted."

Sixteen-year-old Australian actress Bonnie Piesse, cast as Owen's girlfriend, Beru Whitesun, also recognized the significance of re-creating a character who had been established nearly a decade before her birth. To prepare for the role, Piesse viewed all the original *Star Wars* films, which she had seen when she was very young but did not remember well. She reviewed Beru's scenes nearly twenty times, to study the physical mannerisms of Shelagh Fraser, who had first played the role. One of Piesse's main concerns was Beru's American accent—which came from another actress's voice, dubbed over Fraser's for the original film.

"I thought it would be hard to keep up the American accent," Piesse noted, "but when I was on the set, there were a lot of Americans around. So I kind of got into it and found myself speaking in an American accent even when I wasn't filming. I was also nervous about working for George Lucas, because he is so well known. I didn't want to make any mistakes in front of him. Once I got on the set, it was okay, because he was very friendly and nice. In fact, everyone was friendly. It almost felt as if we were filming a home video."

While the young actors tried to tie their performances, to some extent, to those of the original actors in *A New Hope*, Trisha Biggar created a link between Episodes II and IV via the characters' costuming. "Owen's costume is similar to what we see on Luke in Episode IV," she noted. "We also based Beru's costume on the one she wears in Episode IV. George very much wanted to make those

connections in the characters, going forward and backward in time."

In addition to these returning characters, Episode II introduced Owen's father, Cliegg Lars, played by veteran character actor Jack Thompson. Because he was supposed to be an amputee, Thompson wore a blue stocking on one leg from the knee down. ILM later removed the leg by digitally reconstructing, frame by frame, the background behind the blue area. For filming, Thompson sat in a raised chair mounted to dolly tracks, which crew members could push manually.

(Opposite page, top)
Learning that his mother
was taken captive by a band of
Tusken Raiders, Anakin boards a
swoop bike and crosses the Tatooine
desert to find her. (Middle) Anakin
confers with Jawas; Anakin finds
Shmi, battered and bloodied; the
Sand People react to Anakin's
appearance—and
vengeance.

ILM later replaced the rig with the repulsorlift power-chair the character rides in the scene.

L earning that Tusken Raiders have abducted his mother, Anakin sets off that night on Owen's swoop bike, determined to find her and bring her home. His good-bye was shot on the Chott el Jerid, while the subsequent montage of his journey across the desert featured digital backgrounds composited with practical set pieces made up of desert floor, sand dune, and rocky outcrop. Bluescreen elements of Christensen on a bike rig mounted to a gimbal completed the montage.

Under the cover of night, Anakin approaches the Tusken Raider camp, a set that was built and filmed on stage in Sydney the first week in August 2000. To accommodate the camp scene, Bocquet's crew built only two of the Tusken Raider huts—twenty-foot-diameter dwellings made of fabric and mud—while the remainder seen in wide shots were ILM models and CG set extensions. Peter Walpole's crew dressed the interiors of the huts with leather straps, simulated tusks, animal skins, and aboriginal-style carvings. "There were layers and layers of pieces," Walpole said. "It looked rather a mess, really; but I guess Tusken Raiders wouldn't be known for their house pride." A campfire burning between the

(Top to bottom) Anakin makes a pledge to his deceased mother; family members also say their good-byes; the funeral scene behind the scenes.

(Inset, top) **The repulsorlift power-chair ridden by amputee Cliegg Lars—Shmi's husband—was mounted to raised dolly tracks on location and pushed manually.** (Above) **When ILM painted out the rig, the chair appeared to be hovering in midair.**

Pernilla made it that much more emotional for Hayden."

Additional elements for the scene were captured during the second pickup shoot at Ealing. "We were under tremendous time pressure at that point of principal photography," Lucas explained, "so I shot what I could and decided to get the rest later. One of the things I didn't get was Anakin actually coming into the hut, seeing his mother, and then untying her—I had all of that in wide shots, but I didn't have any close-ups. So I did that in October 2001."

Filled with rage at the murder of his mother, Anakin massacres everyone in the camp, indiscriminately killing Tusken men, women, and children. Though we do not witness the slaughter—too dark and violent a scene for *Star Wars*' predominantly young audience—we hear of it in Anakin's later confession to Padmé. Anakin's surrender to his emotions serves as foreshadowing of his ultimate turn to the dark side. "He's too late to save his mother," Christensen observes. "That feeling of defeat tears him apart, and so he goes a bit psycho and murders everyone. That is one of the turning points in his evolution to Darth Vader. I think it is always in the back of his mind that he failed his mother—and that propels him toward the dark side."

After the funeral for Shmi Skywalker back at the homestead, R2-D2 receives an urgent holographic message from Obi-Wan on Geonosis, ominously cut short. Determined to help their mentor and friend, Anakin and Padmé leave Tatooine for Geonosis, where a mysterious ex-Jedi—and a whole lot of trouble—await.

huts—actually a gas flame camouflaged with twigs and logs—completed the set. David Tattersall's lighting crew buried flicker-lamps in the ground, behind and around the campfire, to simulate additional firelight.

Within a Tusken Raider hut, Anakin finds his beaten and tortured mother, Shmi (Pernilla August), but he is too late: Shmi dies in his arms just moments later. The scene between mother and son was a difficult one for Hayden Christensen to play. "When your mom is dying in your arms," Christensen commented, "you want to break down—just cry and bawl and go crazy. But George wanted me to hold back. I think he wanted a later scene, where Anakin breaks down in front of Padmé, to have more impact; and so he had me pull back in this scene."

"There is something about Pernilla August that is hard to explain," Rick McCallum added. "She has an aura about her, and when she walked onto the set, it affected *everybody*. Hayden loved her. Emotionally, this scene is a big turning point, because this is what sets Anakin off. And I think to have the character of his mother played by

132

(Left) Anthony Daniels as C-3PO—sans headpiece—and R2-D2 inside Padmé's Naboo starship. (Below) Drawings and computer renderings of the hologram projector created by Bocquet's production team formed the basis of the physical prop used in the film.

NABOO COCKPIT
HOLOGRAM PROJECTOR . JL 23 VII 00

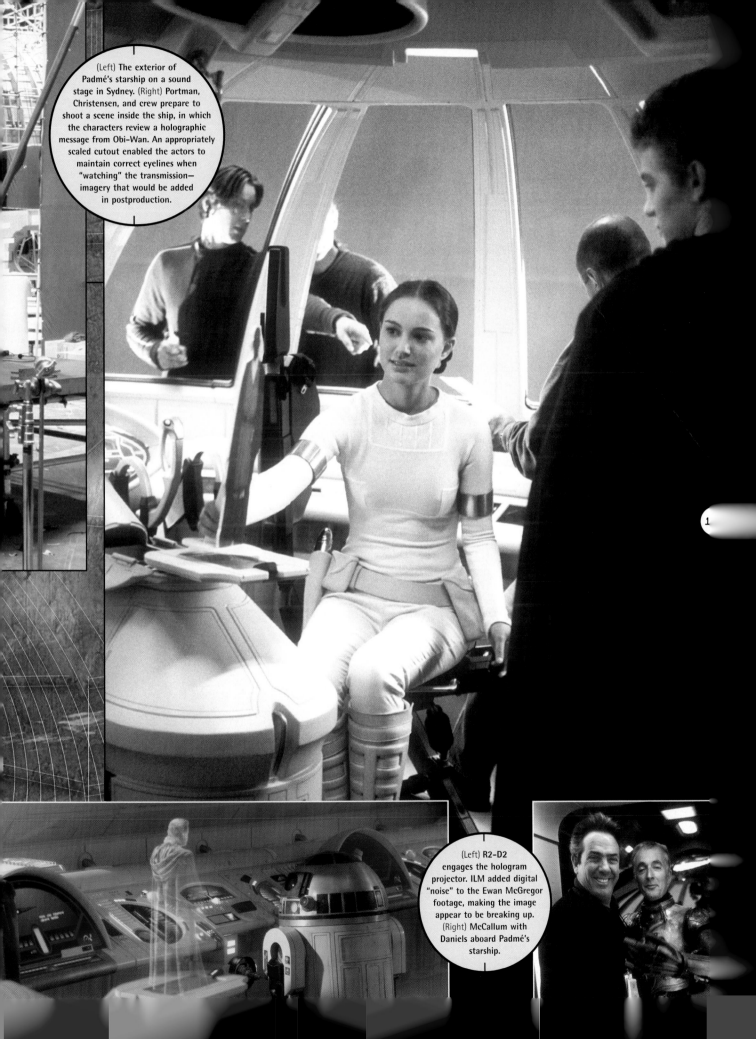

(Left) The exterior of Padmé's starship on a sound stage in Sydney. (Right) Portman, Christensen, and crew prepare to shoot a scene inside the ship, in which the characters review a holographic message from Obi-Wan. An appropriately scaled cutout enabled the actors to maintain correct eyelines when "watching" the transmission—imagery that would be added in postproduction.

(Left) R2-D2 engages the hologram projector. ILM added digital "noise" to the Ewan McGregor footage, making the image appear to be breaking up. (Right) McCallum with Daniels aboard Padmé's starship.

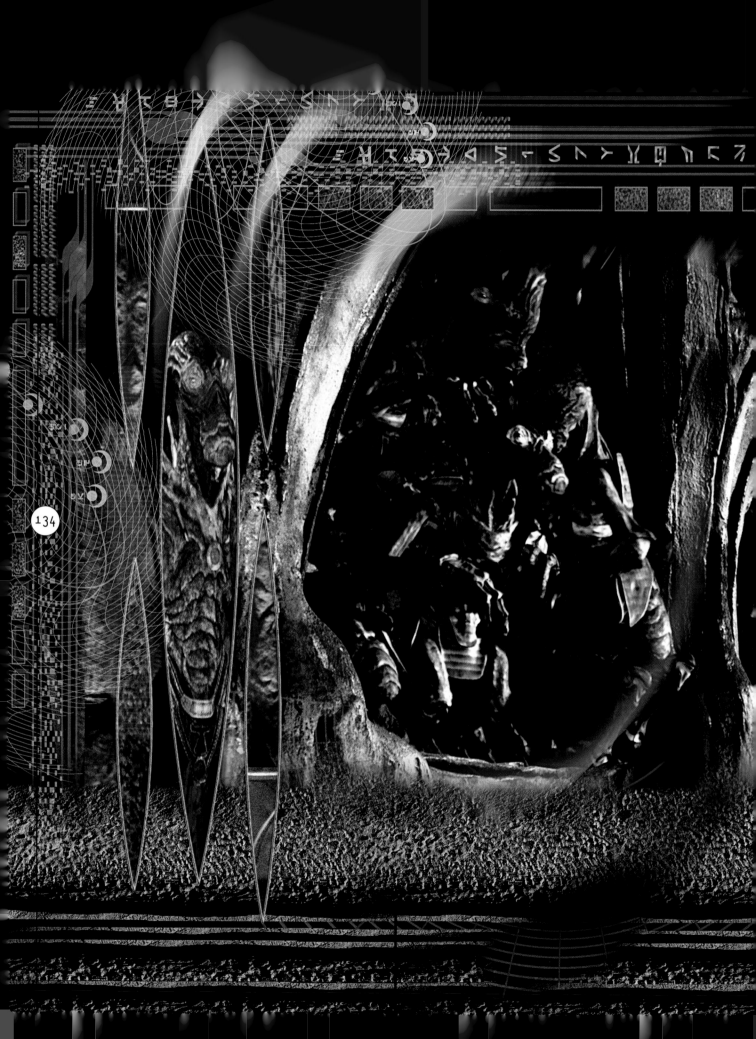

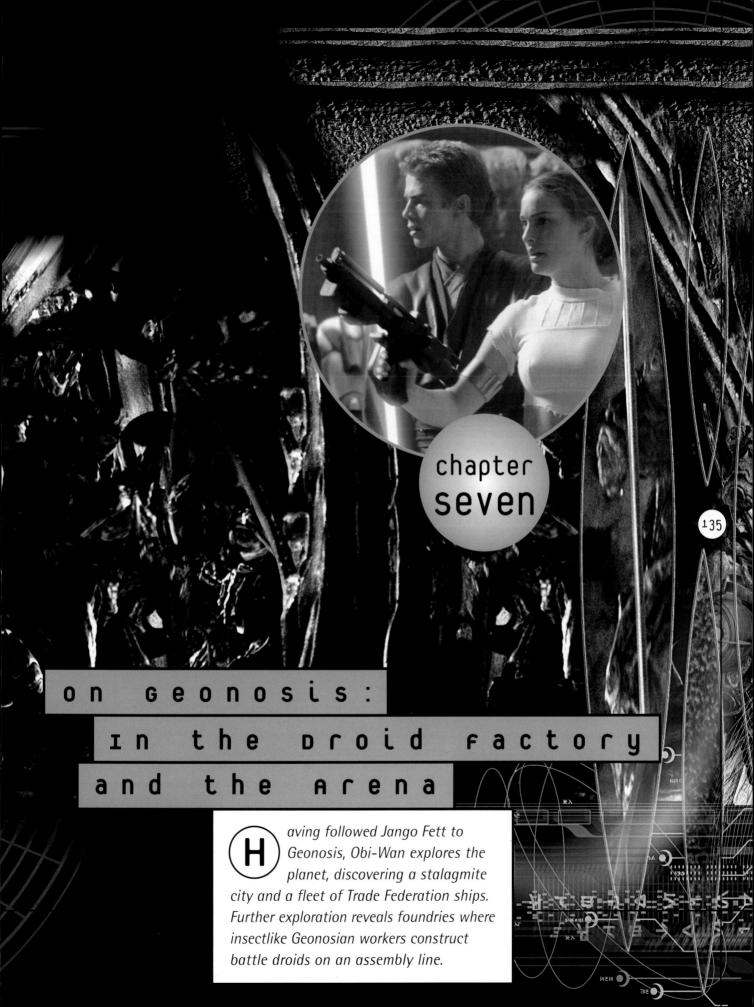

chapter
seven

on Geonosis:
in the Droid factory
and the Arena

H aving followed Jango Fett to
Geonosis, Obi-Wan explores the
planet, discovering a stalagmite
city and a fleet of Trade Federation ships.
Further exploration reveals foundries where
insectlike Geonosian workers construct
battle droids on an assembly line.

Construction crews carve rocklike walls out of foam to create a cavernous environment on Geonosis.

Lucas had envisioned Geonosis as an environment analogous to a termite colony, with cavernous interiors and organic, sculpted rock formations—as if the Geonosians, like termites, have carved out underground chambers. Due to their vast scale, most of the Geonosis environments were created digitally or in miniature; however, Gavin Bocquet's crews did provide small rocklike set pieces, carved out of foam, and a floor of matching-colored sand.

Confronted with sets that consisted of little more than those pieces of carved rock and volumes of draped bluescreen material, David Tattersall relied heavily on illustrations to guide his lighting of the Geonosis environments. "There was a detailed series of paintings by Doug Chiang," Tattersall said, "and those gave us clues as to what those

environments would look like once the CG sets had been composited. These paintings showed them as huge, cathedral-like spaces, with beams of light coming in from high windows. We created those beams on the set with xenon searchlights, mounted in the stage ceiling and bouncing off mirrors to produce the strongest beam. We also filled the stage with smoke to enhance the shaft-of-light effect."

For the look of the computer-generated Geonosians, Lucas started with the original Neimoidian design for Episode I, which had been simplified considerably when time and budget constraints mandated that the characters be played by actors in masks, rather than created through computer graphics. Still fond of the look of the original Neimoidian head, Lucas had it translated to a buglike body, and the Geonosians were born. To guide the concept

(Upper insets) **Obi-Wan's Delta-7 lands on Geonosis.** (Lower insets) Minimal live-action set pieces for the rocky planet were extended with digital and miniature sets. Photographs captured in Utah and stitched together into a panorama served as distant backgrounds. (Bottom of page) **R. Kim Smith and Carol Bauman created sculptures of Geonosis.**

Obi-Wan explores one of the cavelike interiors of Geonosis. In many cases, bluescreen footage of McGregor was composited into miniature rock-formation sets.

illustrators in developing the termite body, Lucas—whose home was besieged by the insects at the time—provided them with live specimens in a jar.

The final creatures were rocky in texture, as if they would blend, chameleonlike, into their natural environment. Lucas also wanted to see distinctions between the upper class and the working class, similar to those in ant and termite colonies: the lower class would be wingless drones, while the upper class would be able to fly. "The royalty class had a double set of wings," Rob Coleman noted, "so it was difficult to work out their flying cycle. They could also hover like dragonflies, their legs hanging down like those of a wasp, to make them look scary."

Overhearing a conversation between members of a nefarious business group that includes Count Dooku, Poggle the Lesser—Archduke of Geonosis (voiced by Marton Csokas)—and Viceroy Nute Gunray (Silas Carson), Obi-Wan learns of a military alliance that has been forged between the Commerce Guild, the Trade Federation, the InterGalactic Banking Clan, Dooku, and the other Separatists. While transmitting a message to Anakin, Obi-Wan is captured and taken to a prison cell, where he finally meets legendary Count Dooku face to face.

Full-scale Geonosian busts as based on the anatomies of termites and ants and sculpted by concept sculptors (left) Robert Barnes and (right) Murnane. The characters' head design was also based on a Neimoidian concept for Episode I. When they became masked rather than CG characters for that film, their heads were simplified considerably. The Geonosians gave Lucas a chance to use that original design, one of his favorites.

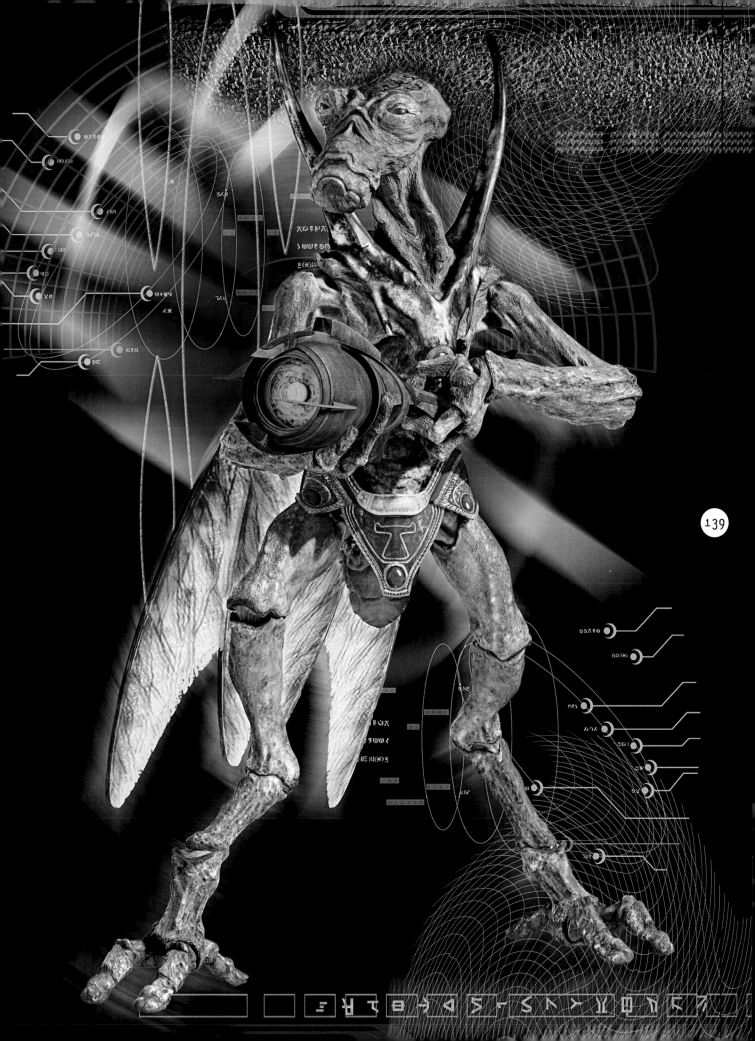

Ex-Jedi Dooku–later revealed to be a Sith Lord, Darth Tyranus–not only served as the movie's principal antagonist, but was also a means for Lucas to illustrate a number of important story points. "I needed to get across the point that Jedi *can* leave the Order," Lucas explained, "to set up what happens with Anakin later on. Also, in the end, when you realize that Dooku is Darth Tyranus, it explains what Darth Sidious did after Darth Maul was killed: he seduced a Jedi who had become disenchanted with the Republic. He preyed on that disenchantment and converted him to the dark side, which is also a setup for what happens with Anakin."

D uring the film's development, Lucas had considered making Dooku a female Sith, and the concept designers had produced numerous drawings to flesh out that idea. Eventually, however, Lucas began to see the character as an elderly, charismatic gentleman with a "Christopher Lee" face; and in one of the film's casting coups, Christopher Lee–star of more than two hundred movies, with a career that has spanned sixty years–agreed to play the role. "I sat down with Christopher and his agent in London," Robin Gurland recalled, "and had the most gorgeous lunch for about three hours. He is such a raconteur, and he carries in his head a wealth of film history. I was completely charmed by the man."

Having Christopher Lee appear in the newest *Star Wars* movie was a wonderfully ironic, "full-circle" situation: Lee had starred with the late Peter Cushing, who portrayed Grand Moff Tarkin in Episode IV, in literally dozens of films during the course of his career–predominantly in horror films of the 1950s. In 1957's *The Curse of Frankenstein*, for example, Lee had played the monster to Cushing's Baron Victor Frankenstein.

As a fan of the original *Star Wars* trilogy, Lee was delighted to join the cast. "That first film was so different

from anything anybody had ever seen," Lee commented. "I was absolutely fascinated by it, and, of course, I saw the next two films as they came out. All of this extraordinary work came out of the mind of George Lucas, and so my feelings toward him were ones of great admiration and respect." Those feelings prompted Lee to say yes when Lucas called him to ask if he might be interested in playing a pivotal role in Episode II of *Star Wars*–even though, since he was still working on the script at the time, all he could

(Left to right) Script supervisor Jayne-Ann Tenggren, Lucas, McTeigue, and Christopher Lee (Count Dooku) go over the script. In the months leading up to the shoot, Lucas had considered making Dooku a female Sith; but eventually he saw the character as an "elderly gentleman with a Christopher Lee face."

tell the actor was that Dooku was a "battle-scarred ex-Jedi."

Lee was on the film for several weeks, and found the experience to be one of the most enjoyable of his decades-long movie career. "When George first called me in London to discuss doing this, he said we'd have a lot of fun–and we did," Lee remarked. "We worked extremely hard, of course, but we were still

Sensing trouble on Geonosis, R2-D2 and C-3PO leave the starship to go in search of Anakin and Padmé.

able to laugh. So much of that is gone in movies now. People are all looking at their watches—time is money, time is money, time is money. There's no time to enjoy yourself. But we had fun on this one. It was also a fascinating experience because I don't often get to work with actors who are nearly sixty years younger than I am."

One of the youngest—thirteen-year-old Daniel Logan, who portrayed Boba Fett—approached Lee on the set one day and asked, "Haven't I seen you in something? I think I've seen you in the movies." The veteran actor looked at the boy casually, smiled, and said, "Well, yes, I've been in *two hundred and forty-seven* movies, so you may have seen me in something."

Confined to a prison cell, Obi-Wan is confronted by Count Dooku in a scene that was written after the end of principal photography and shot in March 2001 at Ealing Studios. In part, the scene was intended to convey expository information about Dooku that had been excised from the earlier scene in the Jedi Temple library. The new scene also allowed the audience to follow what was happening to Obi-Wan on Geonosis.

"In the original script," Lucas said, "Obi-Wan just sort of disap-

peared once he got to Geonosis. The audience didn't know what happened to him. So I thought there was need for a good confrontation scene between Dooku and Obi-Wan. I'd already decided to cut out a scene between Padmé and Dooku—a talky, political, philosophical scene—and that gave me room for this more relevant scene between Obi-Wan and Dooku."

s Obi-Wan is confronted by Dooku in his prison cell, Anakin and Padmé arrive on the redrock planet and go in search of him, leaving R2-D2 and C-3PO within the confines of the starship. In the original script, a small scene took place there between the two droids, with C-3PO pondering the confounding nature of human relationships. The brief scene was shot in a ship's interior set during the third day of principal photography—both R2-D2's and C-3PO's first day of filming for the movie. "That was probably the best day of the shoot for me," Don Bies recalled, "because we were shooting with Artoo and Threepio, back together again in almost their original forms; *and* George was directing again. Everybody was back, so it was an exciting moment.

"At the same time, I approached the day with some dread because, overall, George has the impression that Artoo doesn't work—it just never seems to work when he's around. So here it was the first day of shooting with Artoo

Geonosis is revealed to be the site of a massive droid factory. Battle droids designed for Episode I remained essentially the same for Episode II—except for a more reddish appearance to reflect the rich copper color of the Geonosian soil.

141

Exploring the droid factory, Padmé and Anakin find themselves on a ledge overlooking a deep chasm. Lucas sought to make a number of subtle connections between Episode II and the original trilogy of movies—such as this revised version of Luke and Leia's chasm-swinging scene in A New Hope (inset, below).

attached to that of a battle droid. Farther down the assembly line, the head of a battle droid is attached to C-3PO's body.

Lucas dreamed up the entire droid factory sequence—a major scene in the final movie—in the months following principal photography. "At the end of the movie," Lucas explained, "I originally had three or four very talky scenes. There was a scene where Padmé encountered Dooku and another where Padmé and Anakin were sentenced at a trial. But it became apparent that although Anakin and Padmé were going there on a diplomatic mission to rescue Obi-Wan, the diplomacy angle didn't play very well. We needed some action. At that point, the movie was ready to *go*—and to have people sitting around talking diplomacy didn't work. So I took out all of those scenes and replaced them with an action scene, which is the droid factory.

"Now, when Anakin and Padmé get to Geonosis, they sneak into this factory and wind up fighting the Geonosians. There are still a few talking scenes with Yoda, Mace, and Palpatine on Coruscant—but they are very brief and they are juxtaposed against our heroes, who are in the middle of the action. The droid factory scene also got Artoo and Threepio out of the ship and more engaged in the final act of the movie." Some of the action in the droid factory sequence also served as homage to the original *Star Wars*: at one point, Anakin and Padmé find themselves trapped atop a precipice, much as Luke and Leia were in Episode IV.

As a means of developing the droid factory sequence, previsualization-effects supervisor Dan Gregoire worked closely with concept design supervisors Erik Tiemens and Ryan Church to produce 3D animation. "The factory scene was still fairly loose in George's mind at this point," Rick McCallum noted, "so the animatics guys went off and created this whole sequence—and it was wonderful." The droid factory was filmed during the pickup shoot in March, with

for this movie, and George was there, and I hadn't proven myself yet. Artoo had to go through a doorway that was very narrow—and, sure enough, he bumped into a wall. It didn't hurt Artoo, fortunately, but it did hurt my ego. We did three takes, and on the third take, I got it."

That starship scene between R2-D2 and C-3PO was ultimately dropped. In its place appeared an entirely new sequence in which, sensing trouble, R2-D2 leaves the ship, followed by an exasperated C-3PO, eventually making his way to the factory where battle droids are being manufactured by Geonosian workers. There, R2-D2 comes to the aid of Anakin and Padmé as they fight off attacking, winged Geonosians. Meanwhile, a hapless C-3PO is carried down the factory assembly line, where his head is knocked from his body and

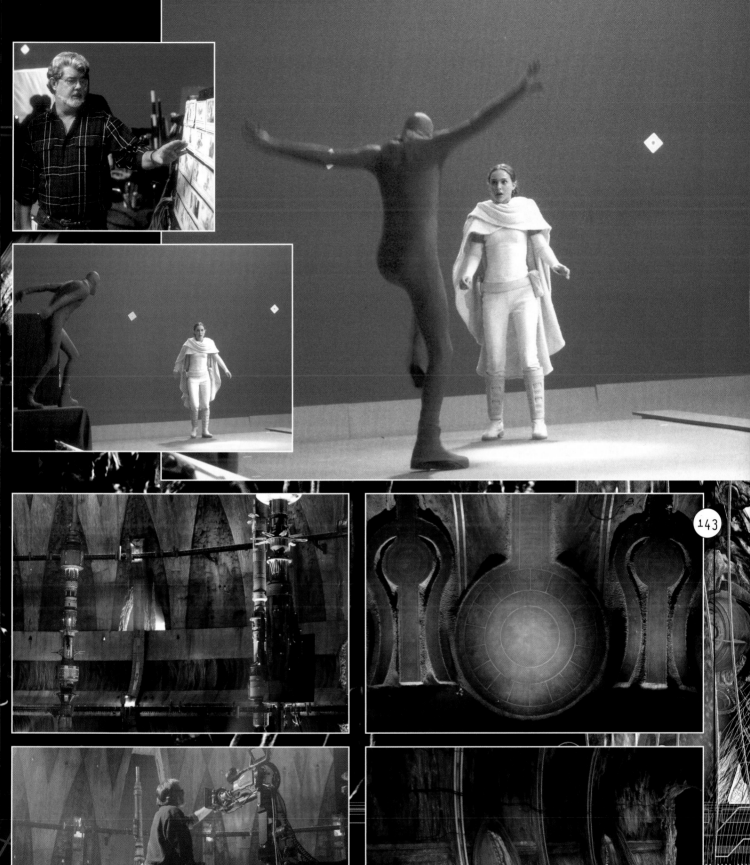
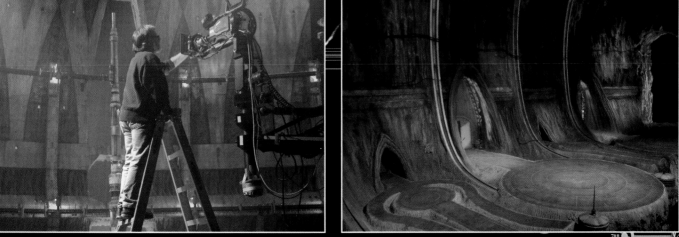

(Above) Because no live-action sets were built for the late-conceived sequence, the entire droid factory environment was realized through miniatures, anamatics, and digital sets—the former for midgrounds and backgrounds, the latter for foreground views. (Right) ILM model maker Charles Bailey puts the finishing touches on a section of the factory miniature. (Below) To capture action of Padmé and Anakin on the factory assembly line, Portman and Christensen were shot running on a conveyor belt on a London blue-screen stage.

(Top) Padmé is sur-
rounded by Geonosians in
the droid factory. (Left)
Separated from Padmé within
the bowels of the factory, Anakin
engages his lightsaber. (Below)
Jango Fett arrives on the scene,
capturing Anakin and Padmé
and delivering them to
Dooku.

146

almost nothing in the way of sets since the scene would rely on computer-generated and model sets matted into bluescreen areas. One doorway was provided, and an all-blue treadmill stood in for the factory's conveyor-belt system—but except for these practical items, the stage in which Natalie Portman, Hayden Christensen, Anthony Daniels, and R2-D2 performed was empty and blue.

(C) aptured by the Geonosians, Anakin and Padmé are sentenced to death—along with Obi-Wan Kenobi—in an execution arena, before thousands of cheering spectators. In a tunnel leading into the arena, certain they are about to die, Padmé finally confesses her love for Anakin. Long after the actors' performances had been shot, Lucas and Ben Burtt continued to tweak the momentous scene in the editing room.

"That moment is very important," Burtt commented. "After this, they fight side by side, but this is their last intimate moment. The way it was written and shot, it was a very long scene, with a lot of dialogue. In the course of editing it, the question came up—do we really need all of this dialogue? We were grappling with other questions, as well. Should the scene be played equally between the two of them, or should it lean toward Anakin? Or should it lean more toward Padmé?"

In the final cut of the movie, much of the dialogue between the characters was omitted. What remained was Padmé stating her love for Anakin simply and plainly. "The scene wasn't written that way," Burtt said, "and it wasn't shot that way; but we restructured it so that she would have the final word, which made a tremendous difference in how it played."

As the seemingly doomed couple kiss, they are led into the execution arena where Obi-Wan is already held captive. Thus begins the film's final act, a nonstop action sequence that segues from a battle between Padmé, Anakin, Obi-Wan, and three arena beasts to a battle between hundreds of Jedi, Geonosians, and battle droids to a full-bore confrontation between battle droids and Republic clone troopers. Like all of the movie's action sequences, the final act was first developed in animatics.

"We kept doing animatics," Lucas said, "then editing them and redoing them. That process went on for more than a year, from the time we finished shooting in September 2000 until end of the year 2001. At that point, ILM took over, creating backgrounds and the final animation, but even

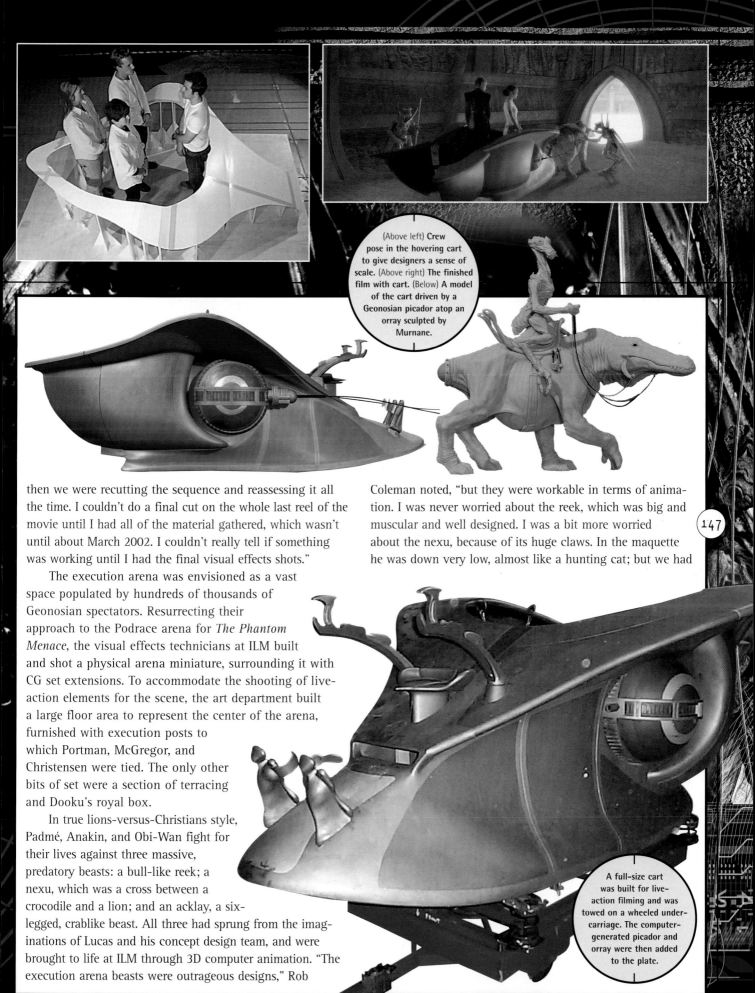

(Above left) **Crew pose in the hovering cart to give designers a sense of scale.** (Above right) **The finished film with cart.** (Below) **A model of the cart driven by a Geonosian picador atop an orray sculpted by Murnane.**

then we were recutting the sequence and reassessing it all the time. I couldn't do a final cut on the whole last reel of the movie until I had all of the material gathered, which wasn't until about March 2002. I couldn't really tell if something was working until I had the final visual effects shots."

The execution arena was envisioned as a vast space populated by hundreds of thousands of Geonosian spectators. Resurrecting their approach to the Podrace arena for *The Phantom Menace*, the visual effects technicians at ILM built and shot a physical arena miniature, surrounding it with CG set extensions. To accommodate the shooting of live-action elements for the scene, the art department built a large floor area to represent the center of the arena, furnished with execution posts to which Portman, McGregor, and Christensen were tied. The only other bits of set were a section of terracing and Dooku's royal box.

In true lions-versus-Christians style, Padmé, Anakin, and Obi-Wan fight for their lives against three massive, predatory beasts: a bull-like reek; a nexu, which was a cross between a crocodile and a lion; and an acklay, a six-legged, crablike beast. All three had sprung from the imaginations of Lucas and his concept design team, and were brought to life at ILM through 3D computer animation. "The execution arena beasts were outrageous designs," Rob

Coleman noted, "but they were workable in terms of animation. I was never worried about the reek, which was big and muscular and well designed. I was a bit more worried about the nexu, because of its huge claws. In the maquette he was down very low, almost like a hunting cat; but we had

147

A full-size cart was built for live-action filming and was towed on a wheeled undercarriage. The computer-generated picador and orray were then added to the plate.

EXECUTION PILLARS

EXTENT OF BUILD ON STAGE
(One full Pillar and two half Pillars)

NOT CORRECT SPACING
BETWEEN PILLARS
WILL BE FURTHER APART

STUNT SET-UP
EXECUTION PILLAR CONFIGURATION

STUNT BOX

STUNT BOX

148

(Top and middle) The execution pillars were erected on a bluescreen stage. (Bottom) As the pillars appear in the film.

(Left) Bocquet's plans for the execution pillars to which Anakin, Padmé, and Obi-Wan are chained. Shorter "stunt boxes" enabled the actors to leap from the pillars without risk of harm.

to lift him up a bit in order to make him work. Also, the walking cycle had the kind of twisting action of a Komodo dragon, and that took some effort. The final monster, the acklay, had fingers coming off its six legs. I wasn't sure what to do with the fingers initially, but overall he moved a lot like a crab."

At one point in the sequence, Anakin is charged by the reek, then jumps onto the animal and rides it, rodeo-style. To simulate the action, Hayden Christensen rode atop a blue-covered, gimbaled construct representing the animal's back,

ultimately replaced with the computer-generated reek. The reek-gimbal ride was the wildest yet for Christensen, who had spent more time than anyone else aboard the rocking-and-rolling motion platform. "There were guys off to the side working wheels that made the gimbal tilt and jerk," he recalled. "My job was just to hold on. I fell off pretty much every take, but I never felt in danger, because Nick Gillard was there looking out for me, and there were mats beneath me on the floor. In fact, it was actually kind of fun to fall off."

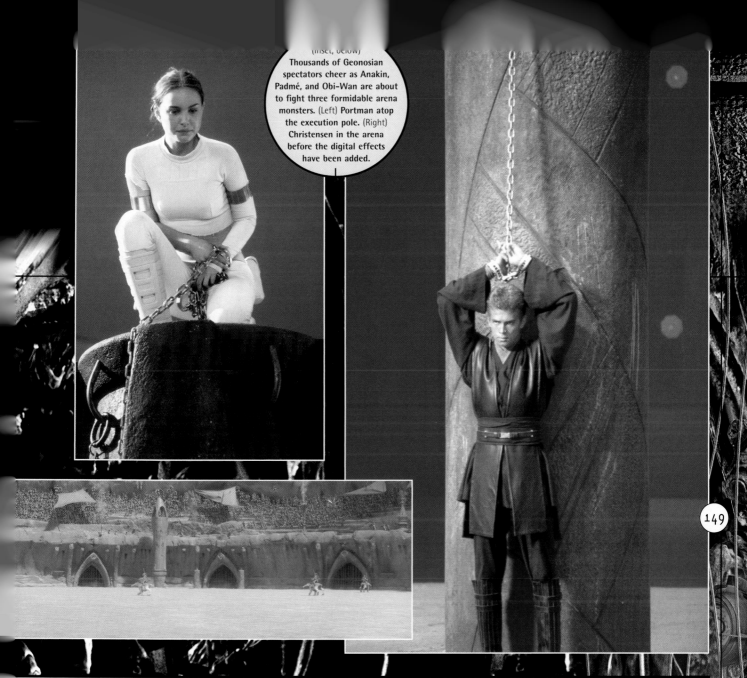

(inset, below) Thousands of Geonosian spectators cheer as Anakin, Padmé, and Obi-Wan are about to fight three formidable arena monsters. (Left) Portman atop the execution pole. (Right) Christensen in the arena before the digital effects have been added.

149

Because Anakin is handcuffed and chained in the scene, Christensen was put into prop handcuffs, from which extended a chain that was screwed to the underside of the gimbal. It wasn't until Christensen's first fall that anyone realized the chain was not long enough to allow the actor to reach the floor—and consequently he was left hanging from the gimbal for a few moments. "I got caught up that first time," Christensen said, "and everyone ran up asking, 'Are you okay?' They were overly cautious, but I guess they had to be."

Natalie Portman, too, performed a number of stunts for the scene, revealing Padmé's more athletic side. "Natalie did quite a bit in that sequence," Nick Gillard noted. "Padmé climbs a huge pole, jumps off it, swings on a chain—and Natalie did all of that herself. She was such a pro, I didn't even have to train her beforehand. We just went through it all the day of, making sure she was safe and that we had crash pads set up for her."

As Obi-Wan, Anakin, and Padmé defend themselves against the arena monsters, Mace Windu appears in the Archduke's box, lightsaber ignited, to confront Dooku and Jango Fett. At his signal, another two hundred Jedi appear around the arena perimeter. The Jedi presence is dwarfed, however, by thousands of battle droids and super battle droids that pour into the arena at Dooku's signal. A huge battle erupts, with Obi-Wan, Anakin, Padmé, and the Jedi attempting to fight off the battle droids, super battle droids, and droidekas. Despite their valiant efforts, the overwhelmed Jedi are soon surrounded, most of their number dead or wounded.

The Jedi battle in the execution arena was a combination of live-action and CG elements. During production, Nick Gillard wrote hand-to-hand combat vignettes for the sequence, then had them committed to storyboards. "Even though a lot of these shots were short little cutaways,"

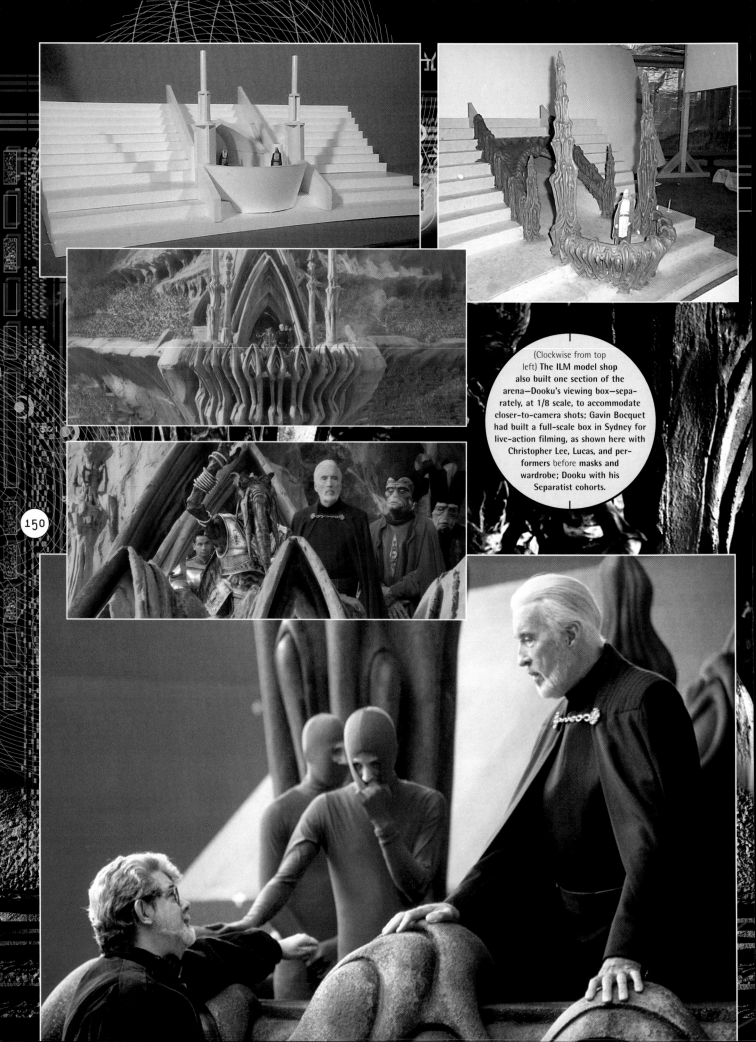

(Clockwise from top left) The ILM model shop also built one section of the arena—Dooku's viewing box—separately, at 1/8 scale, to accommodate closer-to-camera shots; Gavin Bocquet had built a full-scale box in Sydney for live-action filming, as shown here with Christopher Lee, Lucas, and performers before masks and wardrobe; Dooku with his Separatist cohorts.

Even at 1/35 scale, the arena miniature was so large, it had to be built and filmed in eight separate sections. (Inset) The Geonosians were computer generated at ILM, through a custom crowd simulation program. A similar technique had been used to populate the stands for the Podrace arena in The Phantom Menace—but the uneven carved-rock design of the execution arena bleachers made the placement of the CG characters much more difficult.

Gillard recounted, "George wanted each one to be an individual story in itself. I might write, 'Two Jedi fight in the bleachers against a super battle droid.' But then I had to tell a story *within* that little fight: 'The droid fires and blows one Jedi into another, leaps over and cuts his weapon arm off...' et cetera. Each fight had a beginning, middle, and end." The live-action combat vignettes were shot by the second unit at the end of production, as the first unit went on to Tunisia and Italy.

"This was the biggest battle sequence we ever filmed," Gillard noted. "We shot our part with about seventy-five swordfighters and a load of stuntmen. I had to go to countless fencing and kendo schools in Australia to find these people." The stunt performers executed numerous actions for the cameras—falling off walls, jumping into the

air, lightsaber fighting—to provide raw footage. Once assembled into a sequence, that footage was sent to ILM, where digital battle droids, backgrounds, and other effects were added.

In addition to the anonymous Jedi played by stunt performers, the battle sequence prominently featured Anakin, Obi-Wan, and Mace Windu in classic, one-on-one combat with the droids. One of Samuel Jackson's requests to Lucas had been that he be allowed to do some real fighting in Episode II, rather than merely dispense sage advice as he had in Episode I. "I've watched swashbuckling films all my life," Jackson said. "I always wanted to do something like

Arena monsters designed by the Ranch art department included the acklay, a giant creature reminiscent of a lobster or crab. Robert E. Barnes's sculpted maquette (right) served as the basis for ILM's computer model (below).

152

Designed as an extremely low-crouching animal, the computer model for the nexu (below) had to be lifted a bit to help animators create a convincing walk cycle. (Bottom) An illustration of the nexu based on an ILM model.

For the roar of the acklay, Burtt combined a variety of sounds, including primarily the sound of wooden palettes being dragged across the floor (recorded on the set in Sydney) and the clicking sounds of a dolphin. (Insets) The digital evolution of the acklay, picador, and orray.

(Top) John Knoll on the bluescreen stage with Portman and Tattersall in background. For lighting purposes, as seen on computer screens here, stand-ins ride atop a blue-covered reek form mounted to a moving gimbal. (Middle, bottom) In the final shot, the blue form was replaced with the CG reek, with Portman, Christensen, and McGregor—or their digital stunt doubles—astride it.

The Crimson Pirate, with Burt Lancaster swinging from ship to ship and cutting people's heads off with a sword. So I was amped—I wanted to go out and do it." Jackson was granted his wish: The script called for Mace Windu not only to fight droids, but also to go one-on-one with Jango Fett in a centerpiece fight scene.

To prepare, Jackson spent many days in training with Nick Gillard. "Nick put together a very exciting and incredible fight for me," Jackson said. "Since I was supposedly the second baddest person in the galaxy, I dispensed people pretty quickly, using as little energy as possible."

Ewan McGregor's training period with Gillard was relatively short, both because he'd already had extensive training for Episode I and because he was unavailable until after he'd completed the late-wrapping *Moulin Rouge.* Novice Hayden Christensen, however, trained for an entire month before the start of filming. "Hayden and I did two hours of training in the morning and two hours in the afternoon every day," Gillard recalled, "and he was fantastic. He is a hockey player and a tennis player, so he was very athletic, naturally, and he had terrific balance and poise. At one point, he was fighting with the double for Count Dooku, who was the Australian national champion in épée, a style of fencing—but I think Hayden could almost beat him by the time we got to the end of his training."

"Nick is a brilliant man," Christensen said. "He spends hours premeditating how every angle of the lightsaber fights should look; then he picks and chooses from many

september 5, 2000
caserta, italy

The cast and crew arrived by charter plane in Naples, Italy, two days ago, then boarded buses that transported them the twenty miles to Caserta, a city of nearly seventy thousand people, most famous for its eighteenth-century royal palace.

Today, that palace is bustling with film technicians, actors, extras, and excited onlookers. A horse-mounted police force is also on hand to maintain a measure of calm amid the chaos.

(Above) Set dressers retrieved Amidala's throne from Skywalker Ranch, where it had been stored since The Phantom Menace, and then reupholstered it to denote the passage of time and a new Queen. (Left) Hair and makeup personnel prepare Natalie Portman for the throne room scene.

fully ornate stairways, archways, statues, paintings, moldings, and marble floors. The space is so vast, every voice and movement of equipment creates echoes. Set dressers bring in stylized chairs and a crescent-shaped table, which, along with the natural palace interiors, will make up the set for the Theed Palace throne room.

As the set pieces are positioned, George Lucas confers with David Tattersall in a corner.

Minutes later, Lucas looks over the throne room set, repositioning the chairs slightly. Christensen and Portman arrive to prepare for their upcoming scene—Anakin's and Padmé's audience with the Queen upon their arrival in Theed. Portman runs through her lines with the script supervisor.

A number of local young women have been hired to portray the Queen's handmaidens, and Trisha Biggar's crew has dressed them in shimmering, orange-hooded gowns. The first and second assistant directors resort to drawing pictures on paper to communicate with the Italian-speaking extras, explaining their positions and blocking.

Lucas runs through the scene with the principal actors, instructing them to give the Queen a slight bow when they enter the room. They run through it once more, then go off for final hair and wardrobe. The actors come back to the set in costume. Dharker wears an elaborate ceremonial gown.

Lucas shoots the throne room scene, in which the Queen expresses her concern for Padmé's safety; after several takes, he is satisfied. The next setup is a nondialogue, high-angle shot of Anakin and Padmé descending the palace stairs, illuminated by a hovering helium balloon filled with lights. Tired, Portman lies down on the marble steps as she waits between setups. Lucas shoots the action two or three times—and then the crew begins to strike the lights and equipment. At one o'clock in the morning, the shoot at Caserta is completed.

Hayden Christensen, wearing a blue robe, strolls through the exterior palace courtyard, a beautiful, columned expanse filled with birds and a vivid sense of history. In a corner of the courtyard, locals stop to talk and have their pictures taken with Ahmed Best. Natalie Portman, in white robe and running shoes, chats with actress Ayesha Dharker, who is in full ceremonial makeup for her role as Queen Jamillia.

There is bustle inside, as well, where crew members attend to their chores, mostly oblivious to the beauti-

That night, cast and crew board a plane bound for Tunisia, North Africa, across the Mediterranean Sea.

158

(Above right) Storyboards illustrate the charge of the reek, the third arena monster. (Above left) The charge in its final form.

(From top) Lucas confers with Daniel Logan (Boba Fett), who is in Dooku's arena box (Morrison with helmet is in background); Lucas demonstrates Logan's position for when Boba finds his father's helmet; crew and extras await the call to action for the arena battle scene.

159

(Above) Samuel L. Jackson and Christopher Lee on the set between setups. (Below) Lucas talks Jackson—with prop lightsaber—through the scene in which Mace Windu confronts Dooku in his viewing box.

(Left) A crew member preps Jackson for filming. (Below) James McTeigue and Lucas watch as Gillard demonstrates a fencing move for Ewan McGregor.

Lucas based the look of one of the arena Jedi on a Twi'lek named Aayla Secura (Amy Allen), who originally appeared in a Dark Horse Star Wars comic.

Natalie Portman performed a number of her own stunts in the action-packed third act of the movie.

(Left) The battle with the arena beasts erupts into full-scale war with the arrival of two hundred Jedi and thousands of battle droids and Geonosians. Students from Sydney martial arts schools portrayed generic Jedi, while ILM computer-generated all of the sequence's droid and Geonosians. (Bottom) Two Jedi extras, omnipresent bluescreen, and the 24-P camera (right).

different types of martial arts and swordfighting and comes up with the Jedi way of fighting. And it was so cool to do that. It was like being a kid again. The first day I took my lightsaber out on set, I didn't even realize what I was doing, but I made that electronic humming noise—*wwwwoowww*—and then I realized, 'Oh, you guys will put that sound in later, won't you?'"

Anakin's lightsaber was a new design, built by property master Ty Teiger and his department. Though other Jedi would carry standard lightsabers, three new weapons were designed for Anakin, Count Dooku, and Mace Windu. "Count Dooku's was based on a rapier," Teiger explained, "so it actually bent and had a guard on the end of it. Mace Windu's was somewhat funky, with bits of brass and gold, which you've never seen on a lightsaber before. And Anakin's was based on the original Darth Vader lightsaber."

Prototype lightsabers were made out of aluminum, then polished and submitted to Lucas for approval. "Once George had approved the look," Teiger said, "we cast them in resin so we could make multiples, in case of damage. There was a handle and an aluminum rod sticking out of that, painted blue or green or orange so that the actors could fight with it and know what the spatial relationships were." The painted rod was replaced with the lightsaber glow effect in postproduction.

In addition to the well-trained principals and their stunt doubles, the battle sequence featured digital stuntmen, allowing Lucas to let his imagination run wild in conceiving the fights without regard to performer safety or stunt feasibility. "Before, the realities of stunt work always dictated how these things could be put together cinematically," Lucas said. "We'd have to break up stunts into two

Jedi forces go up against not only battle droids introduced in Episode I, but also more powerful super battle droids and destroyer battle droids.

look of wire work. The digital stuntmen allowed me to do the kinds of things I wanted without the onus of wire work and without having to chop things up into three or four different pieces. We were free of physical limitations."

Just as Dooku signals the battle droids to fire on the last surrounded Jedi, six Republic gunships descend into the arena, landing in a cluster around the group. Clone troopers emerge and begin firing on the droids as the surviving Jedi retreat to the ships.

or three shots to get what we needed. The other option was to use a lot of wire work but I don't particularly like the

(Right, middle) With many of their number dead or wounded, the two hundred Jedi are soon overwhelmed by Dooku's numerically superior forces. (Below) Anakin, Mace, Padmé, and Obi-Wan without the digital effects.

Moments later, however, Yoda arrives leading the clone army recruited from Kamino.

167

chapter eight

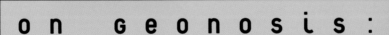

on geonosis:
the clone war
battlefield

Outside the arena, full-blown war breaks out as Republic ships expel tens of thousands of clone troopers, which engage battle droids and Separatist armored vehicles in battle. An aerial skirmish also transpires between Republic gunships and the Geonosian Beak-Wings. Like the final ground battle in The Phantom Menace, the large-scale combat action outside the arena was a nearly all-digital sequence—computer-generated environments, ships, and characters integrated with only bits and pieces of live-action and bluescreen elements.

170

(Insets, above) Concept paintings by Ryan Church and Erik Tiemens of the Clone War: (from left to right) a Republic gunship (Tiemens); a flotilla of gunships (Tiemens); gunships fire on Techno Union ship (Church); Republic craft attack a Trade Federation core ship (Tiemens). (Below) A clash between Jedi and battle droid forces escalates and spreads outside the arena walls when thousands of clone troopers join the fray. Like the final ground battle sequence in The Phantom Menace, the climactic Clone War sequence combined live action with scores of digital characters. All of the action took place in a synthetic environment made up of a forced-perspective ground-plane miniature, mid-ground CG terrain, and background photographic stills.

(Above) **Dooku and his conspirators monitor the progress of the Clone War from a command center.** (Left) A digital rendering of the center.

exchange regarding the *Death Star* plans—added very late in the production schedule and shot in January 2002 at Elstree, during the last scheduled

As war rages outside, Dooku and his allies monitor the advance of the clone army from within a command center, a digital set featuring large, semitransparent maps, a circular viewscreen, and—most notably—a monitor flashing holographic schematics for a familiar-looking, mechanized weapon the size of a small moon. Poggle the Lesser downloads the schematics and turns them over to Count Dooku for safekeeping.

Though the weapon is never mentioned by name in the command center scene, it is clearly the *Death Star*, the "ultimate weapon" against which Luke Skywalker and the entire Rebel army fought in the first *Star Wars*. The small

pickup shoot of the show—was another scene intended to subtly foreshadow the events of the original trilogy, while also adding an intriguing element of nefariousness to Dooku's scheme.

"Once we got the film put together in a form that we could follow from beginning to end," Lucas explained, "it became clear that during the big battle at the end, several of the main characters disappeared for a while—including Count Dooku. So, in looking at that, I decided that I needed to keep Dooku's story going, interweaving it through all the chaos

> **Within the command center, Dooku takes holographic schematics for a familiar looking "ultimate weapon" into safekeeping.**

New ships included the helicopterlike attack gunship as conceived of by Doug Chiang (above left) and Erik Tiemens (above right). Shots of the ships in flight were realized digitally. Medium and close shots of characters inside the gunships were captured on a full-size, practical gunship section, filmed on the bluescreen stage (below). (Bottom) The gunship in an animatic. Due to many long-running and close-to-camera shots, the computer-generated gunship had to be intricately detailed.

174

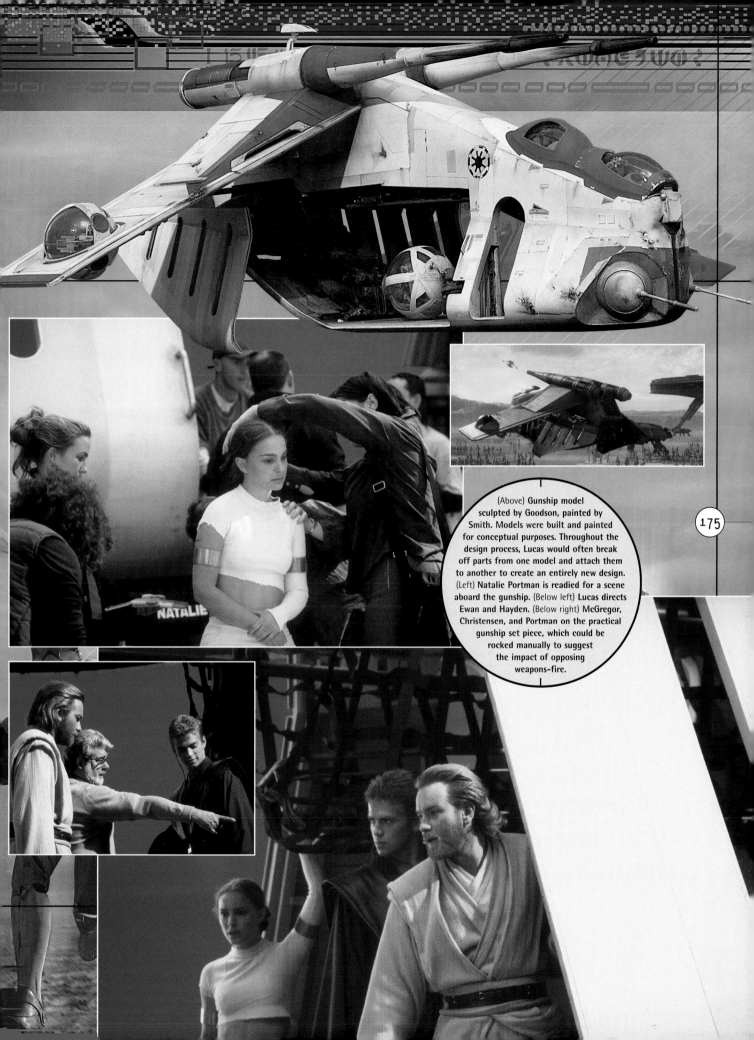

(Above) Gunship model sculpted by Goodson, painted by Smith. Models were built and painted for conceptual purposes. Throughout the design process, Lucas would often break off parts from one model and attach them to another to create an entirely new design. (Left) Natalie Portman is readied for a scene aboard the gunship. (Below left) Lucas directs Ewan and Hayden. (Below right) McGregor, Christensen, and Portman on the practical gunship set piece, which could be rocked manually to suggest the impact of opposing weapons-fire.

As the first Clone War evolved in the editing room from a battle directed by the Jedi primarily from the air to a battle that takes place both above and on the ground, key Jedi—such as Mace Windu and Ki-Adi-Mundi—were given more specific duties on the battlefield.

176

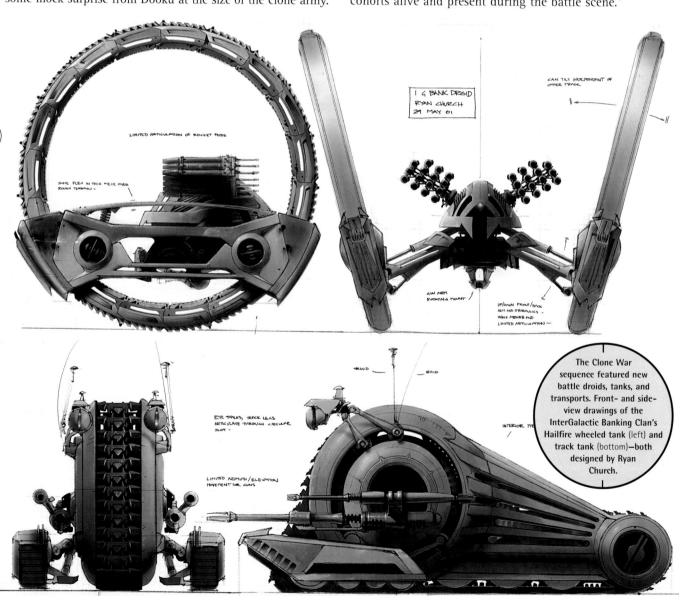

A model and a finished shot of Count Dooku racing toward his secret hangar on a speederbike.

and action of the Clone War. I realized that Dooku probably would have gone to some kind of control center to get an overview of what was going on. I also realized that there should be discussions about how hopeless the battle was, and some mock surprise from Dooku at the size of the clone army.

"And then, by hinting at the *Death Star* plans, I was able to connect this movie to the others. It was a little icing on the cake, but it wasn't really what the scene was about. The scene was about trying to keep Dooku and his cohorts alive and present during the battle scene."

LIMITED ARTICULATION OF ROCKET PODS

SOME FLEX IN THIS PIECE OVER ROUGH TERRAIN –

I G BANK DROID
RYAN CHURCH
29 MAY 01

CAN TILT INDEPENDANT OF OTHER TRACK

GUN ARM ROTATING MOUNT

UP/DOWN FRONT/BACK ARM AND HYDRAULICS – SHOCK ABSORB AND LIMITED ARTICULATION –

EYE STALKS, TRACK LEGS ARTICULATE THROUGH CIRCULAR SLOT –

LIMITED AZIMUTH/ELEVATION MOVEMENT FOR GUNS

RIGID   WHIP

INTERIOR

The Clone War sequence featured new battle droids, tanks, and transports. Front- and side-view drawings of the InterGalactic Banking Clan's Hailfire wheeled tank (left) and track tank (bottom)—both designed by Ryan Church.

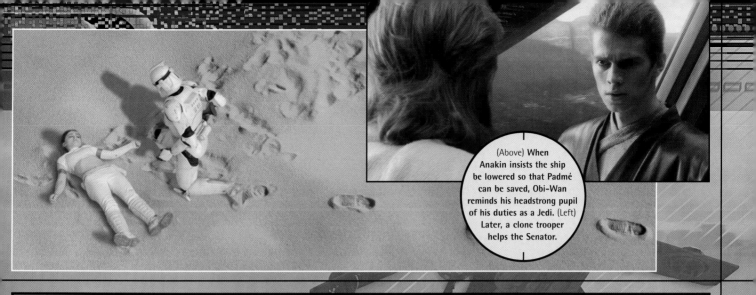

(Above) When Anakin insists the ship be lowered so that Padmé can be saved, Obi-Wan reminds his headstrong pupil of his duties as a Jedi. (Left) Later, a clone trooper helps the Senator.

A s the battle intensifies on the ground, Obi-Wan, Anakin, and Padmé fight off Beak-Wing fire aboard their gunship, which Dooku—now in a Geonosian speeder—targets for destruction. At Dooku's signal, two fighters fire on the gunship, causing it to lurch violently. Padmé tumbles out of the ship, falling to the ground below. Anakin's initial response is to order the ship to land so that he can rescue her; but Obi-Wan reminds him of his duty, going so far as to threaten Anakin's expulsion from the Order if he puts his feelings for Padmé above his duties as a Jedi.

The important exchange between Obi-Wan and Anakin following Padmé's fall from the gunship was also filmed in January, late in the production schedule—although a simplified version of it had appeared in earlier cuts of the film. "It was in that original script, and I shot it," Lucas said, "but it didn't seem to work—mainly because I hadn't written it far enough. I wasn't explicit

enough with the scene. After looking at it, we decided it wasn't strong enough, so we cut it down to nothing.

"But in looking at the movie again, we realized that without that scene, the next scene between Anakin and Obi-Wan, when they confront Dooku, didn't make sense. We'd shot it so there was a lot of anger between them—but without that earlier scene, you don't know where that anger was coming from. So I decided to rewrite that scene and put it back into the movie, but make it stronger and

Also designed by Church, the All-Terrain Tactical Enforcer (AT-TE) was conceived as a precursor to the All-Terrain Armored Transport (AT-AT) featured in The Empire Strikes Back.

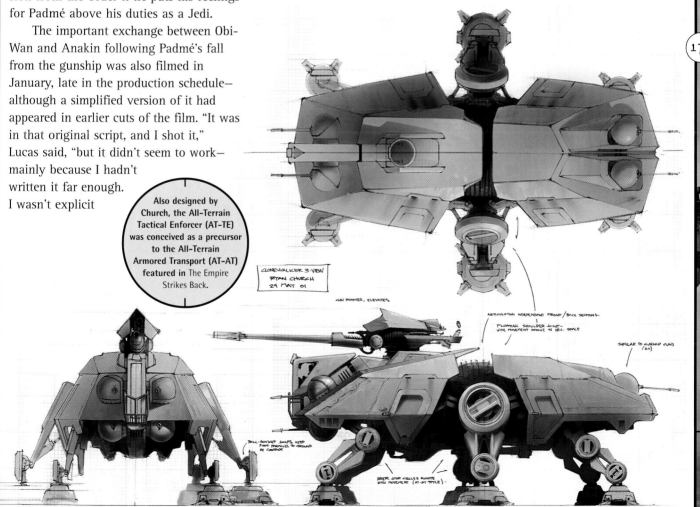

CLONEWALKER 3-VIEW
RYAN CHURCH
29 MAY 01

(Top and bottom)
Final images from the film.
(Middle left, from left to right)
Viewpoint supervisor Jean Bolte, visual effects supervisor Ben Snow, sequence supervisor John Walker, digital effects artist Josh LeBeau, and ILM viewpainter Bridget Goodman. (Middle) Motion capture supervisor Jeff Light and technical animation supervisor James Tooley. (Middle right) Visual effects supervisor Dennis Muren works on the Clone War battle.

(Top) Ground tanks fire on a Trade Federation core ship as it attempts to escape. The effects shot was one of the last finalized by ILM. (Right) Yoda orchestrates the attack from his own command center. (Bottom) Animation provided the laser-like emissions from the ground tanks.

more explicit about what was actually at stake: the fact that Anakin would be kicked out of the Jedi Order if he chose to go after Padmé. I had to make it clear that he had a choice to make. He could either stay in the Jedi Order and go after Dooku, or he could go after Padmé and be kicked out of the Jedi Order."

Realizing that Padmé herself would want him to do his duty, Anakin remains with Obi-Wan in his pursuit of Count Dooku, which leads them to Dooku's secret hangar. The hangar, housing Dooku's Interstellar Sail Ship, was one of the art department's biggest sets, consuming the enormous Stage 2 and rising twenty-five feet into the air. As big as it was, however, the practical set represented only half of the cavernous hangar. The other half was added digitally by ILM.

The ship within the hangar, already called the "Solar Sailer" in Lucas's early drafts of the script, was designed to resemble a giant sailboat. "I'd wanted to do something with Solar Sailers for a long time," Lucas said, "and Geonosis looked like a good culture to fit it into." A large percentage of the ship was built practically because, initially, a fight scene between Dooku, Anakin,

Obi-Wan, and Yoda was going to take place there. The final ship set was approximately seventy feet long, one of the largest fiberglass constructs ever built for a film.

"Gavin had come up with a bold and audacious design for the Solar Sailer," Rick McCallum said, "and it took eight weeks to build it. So everyone was very proud of it, and it was terrible to think of destroying it when we were done shooting. Fortunately, Fox decided to keep it and display it at the studio, which was fantastic."

Obi-Wan and Anakin interrupt Dooku's attempted escape in his ship, engaging him in a lightsaber duel. Hot-blooded Anakin is the first to take on Dooku, but the master duelist quickly dispenses with the boy and takes on Obi-Wan. "One of the problems in writing the Dooku fights," Nick Gillard noted, "was that both Obi-Wan and Anakin had to be master swordsmen—but Dooku had to be even better! It was difficult to make them look outstanding and still make sure Dooku presented enough of a threat that the audience wasn't sure what would happen in the course of the fight. The audience could-n't be certain that Anakin or Obi-Wan would win."

184

T he lightsaber duel made for some of Christopher Lee's most challenging days on Episode II. "I've probably done more swordfights and dagger fights on celluloid than any actor in history," he commented, "but this fight was greater than anything I've ever been involved in. I wasn't able to do that much of it—physically, I couldn't. I'm in my seventy-ninth year, and though my hands and arms still move very fast, my legs don't. So, there are moments where you see me doing certain movements, but only the ones

185

Dooku has dispatched both Anakin and Obi-Wan when Yoda arrives on the scene, prepared to do battle. Lucas had wanted to reveal a more dynamic, powerful Yoda for some time, but had been hampered by the physical limitations of the puppet. The computer-generated Yoda meant that the character could execute fight moves worthy of Bruce Lee, including kicks, jumps, twirls, and midair flips.

Animation direc-
tor Rob Coleman
(bottom) supervised the
creation of the all digital
Yoda. He is shown here with
ILM animation supervisors
Chris Armstrong and
Hal Hickel.

that are not terribly demanding.
Most of it was done by my stunt
double, who was superb. He'd
perform these incredible patterns, and then, at a chosen
moment, I would step in." In
many shots, ILM digitally
replaced the stunt double's face
with Lee's to complete the
illusion. "By the time they were
done with it, it looked as if
Christopher Lee, as Count
Dooku, had engaged in one of
the greatest fights ever seen
on the screen."

187

Anakin jumps back into the fray with Dooku after
Obi-Wan is injured. Within moments, however, the Padawan
is again outmaneuvered, and in one quick move of his
lightsaber Dooku cuts off Anakin's arm at the elbow. Anakin's
death is imminent—but then the diminutive figure of Yoda
emerges through the hangar's entrance.

In a *Star Wars* first, the ancient Jedi Master proceeds
to display his stunning Force and lightsaber skills
against Dooku—a historic lightsaber duel made possible by a computer-animated rather than puppeteered Yoda.
"I had a visual concept for the Yoda and Count Dooku fight
in my mind for a long time before we did it," Lucas commented, "but I didn't know how well it would work. It was
one of those situations where we set ourselves an impossible
task and then just hoped we could accomplish it."

"One of the longest conversations I had with George
about this movie concerned that fight between Yoda and
Count Dooku," Rob Coleman recalled. "We had discussions
about how Yoda would move—was it going to be reminiscent of martial arts or something else? We also talked at
one point about his standing stationary in the room and

using only the Force to fight Dooku, but George wanted
him to be more active than that. He wanted to show this
more powerful, physical side to him. But until it evolved, it
was difficult to visualize a fight between these two unlikely
adversaries: an eighty-year-old man who was about six foot
five, and an eight-hundred-year-old creature who was
three feet tall."

Though the Dooku–
Yoda fight became the
movie's most crowd-pleasing
moment, in its long development
phase the filmmakers agonized
over how to create a convincing
lightsaber duel between the
elegant, six-foot-five Count and
the ancient, frail-looking,
diminutive Jedi
Master.

At age 79, Christopher Lee was in tremendous physical shape—but still needed the help of cinematic trickery to pull off his dynamic and athletic lightsaber duels. Lee performed the parts of the fight he could, and then his stunt double stepped in. To better sell the illusion, the stunt double's face was digitally replaced with Lee's visage in a number of shots.

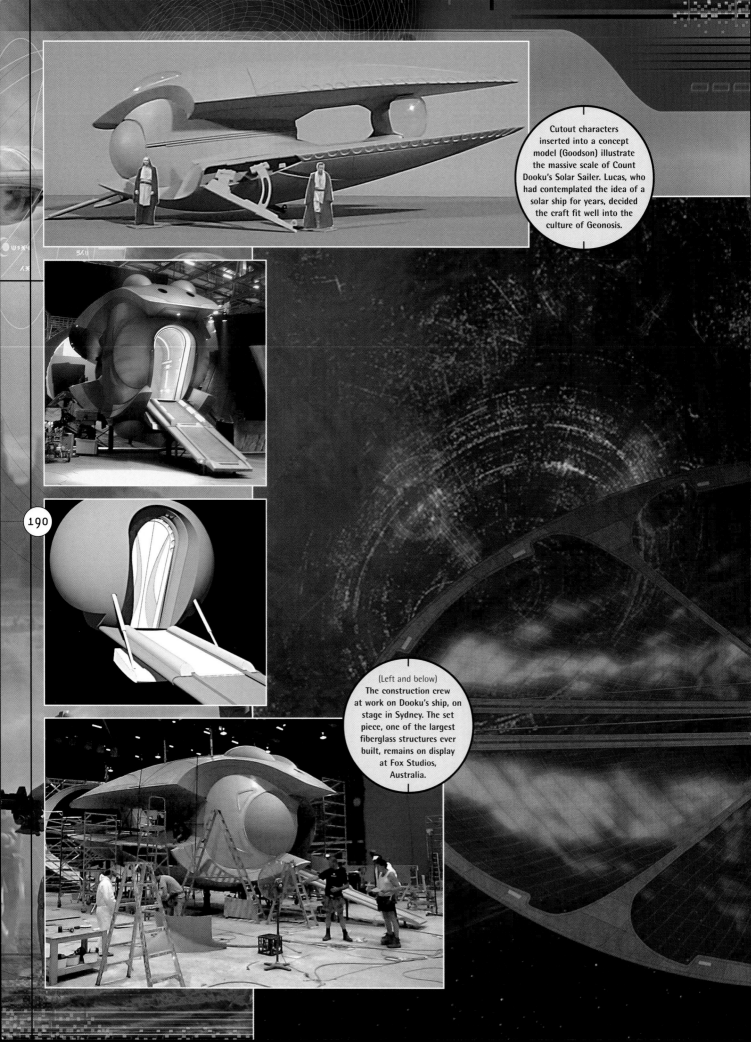

Cutout characters inserted into a concept model (Goodson) illustrate the massive scale of Count Dooku's Solar Sailer. Lucas, who had contemplated the idea of a solar ship for years, decided the craft fit well into the culture of Geonosis.

(Left and below) The construction crew at work on Dooku's ship, on stage in Sydney. The set piece, one of the largest fiberglass structures ever built, remains on display at Fox Studios, Australia.

The
Solar Sailer in
flight. (Above)
McCallum and Lucas on
the set in Sydney (focus
puller Brett Matthews
is in the back-
ground).

september 20, 2000
Elstree Studios, London

This is the last day of principal photography. A month ago, hundreds of performers, designers, and technicians bustled though Sydney's Fox stages; today, the crew has been whittled down to a couple dozen, and Ewan McGregor is the only actor present. The venue, too, has changed, production having moved to Elstree Studios in London a little more than a week ago.

Final shots of principal photography involved Obi-Wan's flight from Padmé's apartment while holding on to an assassin droid. Ewan McGregor was shot blue-screen, hanging from a crane. ILM added the CG droid and cityscapes in post-production.

The crew is set up on a blue-screen stage to film Obi-Wan holding on to a flying droid for the airspeed chase sequence. McGregor stands on a blue-covered floor beneath a prop droid that is also covered in blue, hanging at the end of a crane arm just high enough to enable the actor to reach up and grasp it with both hands. As a huge wind machine blows his hair and clothing, McGregor bends his knees and sways back and forth, as if hanging on to the airborne droid. Interactive lighting flashes on the actor's face from time to time, as if he is passing in and out of darkness. He mimes the cutting of wires, moves his feet as if running across an imaginary rooftop, then releases the droid, dropping out of frame to the floor.

That done, the crew moves on to a scene in which Obi-Wan reacts to Zam Wesell firing on him. After rehearsing the action a few times, Lucas is ready to

capture it on camera—the last shot of principal photography. It is a significant moment, and, as is customary, McCallum will call the shot himself, clapping the slate in front of the camera lens just prior to "Action"—just as he did for the *first* shot of principal photography. It is a beginning and ending ritual McCallum and Lucas have observed on every project since the start of their producer–director relationship. But McCallum has stepped out; and so, after looking around for him briefly, Lucas picks up the slate and faces the camera. "We waited for you, Rick," he says into the camera as he raises the slate, but just at that moment, McCallum hurries onto the stage to perform the ceremonial task himself.

For this final shot, McGregor is again holding on to the droid as the wind machine blows toward him—but this time the camera is mounted on a crane arm that moves up from the actor, then around to capture a high-angle shot from behind. Lucas calls, "Cut." If all has gone well, the shoot is now over.

But visual effects supervisor John Knoll points out trouble—the blue sleeve on the crane arm moved up a bit in the wind, exposing the metal beneath. Lucas turns to the crew and says, "We're going to try one more." There are a few groans of disappointment.

They do it again.

The wind machine is cranked up to a higher speed. McGregor bobs and weaves. The camera moves up and around to the actor's back. Lucas calls out, "Cut. Beautiful. That's a wrap!"

The crew erupts in whistles and applause. Lucas, McCallum, and McGregor exchange celebratory hugs and slaps on the back.

Principal photography on *Star Wars*: Episode II *Attack of the Clones* is over.

193

(Above) After fleeing Geonosis, Dooku arrives on Coruscant. (Left) Dooku meets with his Master, Darth Sidious, whose former apprentice (right), Darth Maul, was dispatched by Qui-Gon in Episode I.

Clone troopers amass for the great Clone War. Because not a single clone trooper suit was built for the film, every helmeted and armored trooper—even those close to camera—was computer-generated. ILM staffers performed marching moves on the motion capture stage as a means of animating the thousands and thousands of digital characters.

194

Republic officials watch from a Senate building balcony as the clone army assembles below. The balcony had been built as part of Padmé's apartment set; but when it proved unnecessary, Lucas suggested its use in this dénouement shot on Coruscant. Only Palpatine and Bail Organa were actually filmed on the set piece. Additional characters in masks were shot bluescreen at ILM, then composited into the live footage, along with a matte-painted view of the transport area. With the exception of The Empire Strikes Back (1980), Star Wars films often end with a display of pageantry: (clockwise from top-left inset) The Phantom Menace (1999), A New Hope (1977), Return of the Jedi (1983).

197

Clearly outskilled by Yoda, Dooku distracts the old Master by using the Force to topple a crane onto the disabled Obi-Wan and Anakin. As Yoda concentrates on suspending the crane in midair, Dooku escapes in his Solar Sailer. Both the crane and the departing ship were computer-generated.

In one of the film's final scenes, Dooku lands his spacecraft in a secret hangar in Coruscant, where he meets with Darth Sidious to report the start of the Clone War. To accommodate the scene, Bocquet and his crews replaced the Geonosis hangar floor around the full-scale Solar Sailer with more Coruscant-appropriate flooring. "Rather than moving the Solar Sailer," explained Bocquet, "we just changed the set around it—that ship was so big, it would have been harder to move that than it was to just change the flooring."

V iews of surrounding Coruscant were digital matte paintings. More digital images made up a following scene in the Coruscant military staging area, where Palpatine, Bail Organa, and Mas Amedda, standing on a balcony, watch tens of thousands of clone troops file into Republic assault ships. The balcony was actually a re-dressed set piece originally built for Padmé's apartment. "George had wanted this balcony for Padmé's apartment," Bocquet recalled, "but when he was filming there, he could never find a reason to use it. So, rather than waste it, he said: 'Why don't we use it for the balcony scene at the end of the movie?' And that's what we did. We shot Palpatine and Bail Organa and Mas Amedda watching this final

scene from that balcony—cue the music, cue the twinkle in the Chancellor's eye!"

In a wordless coda to *Star Wars: Attack of the Clones*, Anakin and Padmé marry privately before a holy man in a rose-covered arbor at the Naboo lake retreat. The wedding scene was shot at Villa Balbaniello, after a day of torrential downpour. As if nature itself was blessing this union, the stormy skies parted and the sun came out—beautifully and miraculously—for the two hours it took to film the small ceremony.

The scene, though brief, gave Trisha Biggar and her costume crew an opportunity to create a stunningly beautiful wedding gown for Padmé. "The wedding dress was very important," Biggar noted. "But since it was a private wedding, George didn't want the dress to be too grand or elaborate. He wanted simple shapes and clean lines, with a slight Edwardian feel."

Dissatisfied with the laces and fabrics she had culled from all over the world, Biggar wound up creating the dress out of a hundred-year-old bedspread. "We found the bedspread in an antiques shop in Australia," Biggar said, "and we incorporated the panels of that with a very fine embroidered silk net. It was off-white, and because it was on such fine net, you could see through it to areas of the skin. The final effect was a gown with very simple lines, with an antique feel to it, but at the same time it was quite intricate, and you couldn't quite put your finger on what it was made of." Portman also wore an Edwardian-style headdress and veil in the wedding scene.

The newly married couple kiss, an appropriately romantic ending to this most darkly romantic episode of the *Star Wars* saga.

Wardrobe and makeup crews prepare Christensen and Portman for the wedding scene, shot in Lake Como, Italy, at the Villa Balbaniello. Though it had rained for most of production's time there, the sun came out for this scene.

199

In an arbor overlooking the sparkling lake, Anakin and Padmé take their vows before a Naboo holy man—behind the scenes (above) and in two final shots (top and middle inset). At the eleventh hour, Lucas decided to film Padmé taking Anakin's mechanical hand. Only those who saw the film projected digitally saw this shot.

BACK TO THE RANCH

P rincipal photography ended in England on September 20, 2000. *Having endured a year of preparation, sixty shooting days, and thousands of travel miles, Lucas and McCallum returned to Skywalker Ranch. Lucas's priority upon his return was to assemble a first cut of the film with Ben Burtt, a process that would take several months. They would be the most enjoyable months of the entire production for Lucas.*

(Above) Skywalker Ranch. (Left) Burtt at the Avid, a digital editing system that allows for quick and easy access to any take of any scene. Burtt had assembled a rough cut of the film during principal photography to give the live-action material a basic structure, but the task was essentially started from scratch when Lucas returned. (Right) McCallum at the Main House.

"My heart is actually in the editing room," Lucas admitted. "When I'm shooting, I'm just gathering material so that I can go into the editing room and have a good time. Many people come up with an idea, they plot everything out, and then they religiously follow that rigid matrix that they've set up for themselves. But I don't like to do that. I like a film to be organic; I like it to change. So I catch a lot of material, let all kinds of funny influences come into it, and *then* I cut."

Burtt had actually put together a rough cut of the film during principal photography, assembling dailies—the footage captured on any given day—as they came in and incorporating notes from Lucas. Still, while that rough cut gave the potential film some form and structure, Lucas and Burtt virtually started from scratch when they sat down at the editing suites in the Ranch's Main House.

"After the shoot, we came back to the Ranch and George sat down with me and watched what I had done," Burtt recalled. "At that point he began to impose his own ideas on every shot—sometimes on every *pixel* of every shot." The mechanics of the editing process were the same as those established by Lucas and Burtt in their previous collaborations. Typically, Burtt would present Lucas with a few-minutes-long cut of a particular scene, and the two of them would discuss that scene in its current state. All of the scenes, and all of the takes for every scene, were easily accessed, as the pair worked on an Avid digital editing system.

"We had access to everything that was shot," Burtt explained, "and we could call up any take within seconds, so we could very quickly find any take George wanted to review. Sometimes he'd look at a cut of a scene and say, 'Let's see what else we've got.' So we'd call up the dailies

In the art department of Skywalker Ranch, Dan Gregoire creates animatics for shots in the Clone War sequence.

for that scene, and that would refresh his memory as to what he shot. Then, based on his review of the material, he'd start reworking the scene."

Another of Burtt's responsibilities was to build up temporary elements that would help Lucas visualize shots that would not be final until ILM had completed its visual effects. The technique was an extension of the videomatics Burtt had created at the beginning of the project. "Sometimes the actors were on only a partial set, or were entirely surrounded by blue," Burtt noted, "which made it hard to determine whether or not a shot was working. So I made up rough versions of those visuals."

Just as he had done for the videomatics, Burtt gathered sketches, storyboards, and paintings from the art department, as well as images of clouds, mountains, landscapes, and skies from the stock footage library. "Using that material," Burtt said, "I'd build up a bluescreen shot, putting our actors against those backgrounds just to put the shot in some kind of context. If there were going to be CG characters in the shot, I would take drawings of those characters, cut them out, and then animate them into the scene. Sometimes I'd shoot video of somebody in costume and put that element in—anything to give us an idea of what a final shot might look like."

T he first cut was completed around the middle of February 2001, at which point Lucas, Burtt, Rick McCallum, and a handful of others watched, for the first time, the entire film from beginning to end, rather than in ten- and twenty-minute increments. "My reaction to those first viewings is always disappointment," McCallum admitted. "All I see are the things that are wrong, the lost opportunities—why didn't we do this or that? Before you see the entire movie for the first time, you are still in the realm

of fantasy. But when you finally see it, you hit the reality wall real hard."

Based on that initial viewing, Lucas determined what was needed to clarify the story, what scenes were not entirely satisfactory, and what scenes were unnecessary. "That first cut was about three hours long," Lucas said, "so the next step was to cut out a lot of the material that seemed redundant. When you are writing a script, in order to make a point, you make the same point three times, hoping that it will register with the audience. But when you see the film, you realize that you don't need to make that same point three times—you can get away with two times, or even mentioning it only once. But you can only determine that after you've seen the film and seen how the impression is made in the context of the whole movie.

"So the first thing I did was go through and take out the things that were redundant. Then I went through and tightened up the scenes that were still there, taking out unnecessary dialogue, unnecessary establishing shots—all the things that slowed down the pace—until it was as tight as I could make it."

"George came into the editing room with the attitude that nothing was sacred," Ben Burtt added. "He looked at it as an audience would, and was very critical of it. If a line of dialogue didn't work, he threw it out. He wasn't unduly attached to anything. Once in the editing room, he was very free in throwing out anything he thought was 'wrong' or unnecessary."

The next step was to assess what elements were missing from the story. "There were cases where scenes were taken out because they weren't necessary to the whole of the film," Lucas explained, "but they might have contained pieces of information that we needed and now had to be put back in somehow. I began looking for anything that was unclear or needed to be amplified. And at that point, I wrote new scenes to fill in those spots."

A scaled-down film crew subsequently captured those new shots and scenes at Ealing Studios, in London, in March 2001—the first in a series of three pickup shoots that

november 6, 2001
ealing studios, london

More than a year has passed since the end of principal photography, and George Lucas, Rick McCallum, and a scaled-down crew are back in England for the second of three pickup shoots. They have been here more than a week, and this is the last day scheduled for this shoot.

First up this morning is a new scene between Anakin and Obi-Wan, set in the elevator leading up to

In a scene added more than a year after the end of principal photography, Anakin and Obi-Wan exchange friendly banter as they ride an elevator to Padmé's penthouse suite.

Padmé's apartment on Coruscant. Lucas has added light banter between mentor and student, to better establish their close and amiable relationship—something he found lacking in the original introduction that had been scripted for the duo, which was a sniping exchange within the apartment.

Ewan McGregor and Hayden Christensen stand on a bluescreen stage to perform the elevator scene. McGregor has just come off filming director Ridley Scott's *Black Hawk Down*, for which his hair was cut military short, so the hairdressers have had to re-create the look of his formerly long hair with a wig.

To create the impression of an elevator rising between floors, director of photography David Tattersall has mounted a fan to break up a key light in a repeating

cycle. During a test run, however, Lucas decides that the fan is too small, making the light flicker too rapidly. "It looks like the elevator is going up too fast," he says. There is no other fan available, and so Lucas and Tattersall think for a moment. "Can you put flags on the blades to make the fan bigger?" Lucas finally asks.

"Yeah, we can do that," says Tattersall, who immediately sets off to make the adjustment.

During the wait, stunt coordinator Nick Gilliard—who has been jovial all day—tells jokes and bursts into a spirited rendition of "Michelle," singing the entire first verse in French.

The elevator scene is ready for rehearsal at 8:30 a.m. By 8:45 a.m., Lucas has captured five takes and is ready to move on. "That's all for Hayden," first assistant Richard Hewitt announces, and everyone applauds and shakes hands with the young actor, who can now return home until he is called for the next round of pickups, in January.

McGregor still has several pieces, shot throughout the morning and early afternoon. His last shot—and the last of this pickup shoot—is a lunge over the landing platform on Kamino, during his fight with Jango Fett. Lucas had filmed the action leading up to the lunge during principal photography, and a digital stunt double of Obi-Wan will pick up the action after his fall; but the lunge itself is a missing piece. Appropriately, McGregor's last line of the shoot is, "I have a bad feeling about this"—a line that has been featured in every *Star Wars* film so far. (This line was subsequently changed to "Not good." The "bad feeling" line is later said by Anakin in the arena.)

After a few rehearsals and even fewer takes, Lucas is satisfied.

"Cut. I think we're done," he says; then, amid congratulations, he autographs Episode I DVDs and photographs for the British crew.

Rather than shoot the entire movie during principal photography, Lucas—as he has always done—broke up shooting over many months. The approach enabled him to look at the movie in its current state, determine what was missing, then go back in to shoot those missing elements, such as additional shots for the droid factory sequence and of Portman.

would take place over the course of the next year. "All of my films have been structured so that I shoot, then come back and edit and rewrite, then go back and shoot some more," Lucas said. "I then cut it again, rewrite it again, and come back and shoot again. I usually have at least two or three additional shooting sessions after the main unit has finished. Those sessions are planned and budgeted, and they're part of our contracts with the actors. It is just like a normal production, except that instead of filming the whole thing in one period of time, it's broken up into these segments."

"What George wants to do in principal photography," Rick McCallum added, "is just get the bulk of the material—then worry about the detail later, in editing. He's like a painter who goes in, paints, steps back, then goes back in. But you can only do that if you set up the production the way we do, with a principal photography schedule, followed months later by multiple pickup shoots."

Among the scenes shot at Ealing the last week in March and the first week in April 2001 were the droid factory sequence, Anakin and Padmé in the Naboo starship, various pickups for the arena battle, the remainder of the fight between Obi-Wan and Jango, Anakin's approach toward the Tusken Raider camp, and additional shots for the Theed Palace throne room scene. In addition, the crew shot the new ledge scene between Jango Fett and Zam Wesell, a new scene in Palpatine's office, and a new Jedi Council scene in which Obi-Wan and Anakin receive their Padmé-related assignments from Yoda and Mace Windu—all written after the end of principal photography.

Upon his return to Skywalker Ranch that spring, Lucas incorporated the new material into the film, then clarified once again what small pieces were missing, in preparation for yet another shoot at Ealing the following October and November. Lucas, like everyone else, had no idea how the

207

Shots of Anakin on the swoop bike on Tatooine were also captured long after principal photography, on stage in London. The giant fan in front provided the illusion of speed.

ILM visual effect supervisors Pablo Helman (left) and Ben Snow (right).

world would change in the months between those two pickup schedules. Six weeks before the production's autumn shoot at Ealing, four hijacked planes became the instruments of the worst terrorist attack ever perpetrated on the United States.

An overall anxiety about flying followed, delaying and even halting some film productions as actors and crew members decided to stay home rather than risk the airways. "Dozens of pictures closed because of it," Rick McCallum said. "We didn't close, but we had to be sensitive to the fact that some people were freaked out about traveling. I called the actors and offered to drive them up to Canada so they could fly out of there if they wanted. No one took me up on the offer, but they were glad to have the option, and there was no problem."

Whereas the spring shoot had consumed twelve days, the fall shoot was scheduled for only six, and was devoted to brief pickup shots for the final battle with Dooku; Shmi Skywalker's death scene; the Jedi battle on Geonosis; the homestead dinner on Tatooine; scenes with Mace Windu, Obi-Wan, and Yoda walking the Jedi Temple corridors; a new scene between Anakin and Palpatine in the Chancellor's office; and the new elevator scene with Obi-Wan and Anakin. In all of the pickup filming, production made do with as little set construction as possible, relying on ILM to fill in the missing environments with digital sets.

November also saw a number of automated dialogue replacement, or "ADR," sessions at a recording studio in London's Soho district. The ADR process has the actor standing at a mike, facing a large-screen projection of the movie. A scene is played one phrase or sentence at a time, so that the actor can re-create his on-set vocal performance, synchronizing it with the movements of his lips on the big screen. Though it is typical for much of any movie's dialogue to be re-recorded in a studio—due to the contamination of on-set production sound—an action-oriented, effects-laden film such as *Star Wars* is particularly dependent on ADR.

"In these kinds of movies, there are big fans or rain machines going all the time," explained Matt Wood, who conducted the ADR sessions with Lucas. "There are also a lot of situations where characters are supposed to be walking on metal floors of ships or platforms—but the sound isn't right because those floors are actually made of creaking wood. So, typically, we replace eighty-five percent of the dialogue."

The digital cameras added another wrinkle. "Some of the equipment related to the high-definition cameras emitted a noise that compounded the production sound problems," Wood noted. "Film cameras are noisy, too—but this was a broadband noise that was at the same frequency as the human voice. That meant that we couldn't filter out the noise without filtering out the dialogue, as well."

ADR had actually started at Ealing during the previous March pickup schedule, in a room Wood converted into a recording studio. At that time, Wood and Lucas recorded the dialogue for many of the computer-generated characters, providing ILM animators with vocal performances on which to base their animation. Other digital characters were recorded at Skywalker Sound, via a digital line to Sydney. "Since a lot of the actors were in Sydney and New Zealand, halfway across the world, it was easier to record them by setting up a remote link between the actors and the Ranch than to fly over there," Wood explained. "We both had the same video source material, so we could see the video at both ends for synching purposes. We would hear it as they were performing their lines, so George could judge the performance quality and I could judge the syncing, the projection levels, and so forth. They would record it there, save it as a digital file, and then send that file to me over the Internet about an hour after the session was completed."

In November, the venue for the ADR sessions moved from the converted room at Ealing to the Soho recording studio. There, Ewan McGregor did two full days of ADR, painstakingly re-creating and re-recording nearly every line of his dialogue in the film. The process was faster and less taxing for Anthony Daniels, whose C-3PO had

no moving lips with which he had to sync his dialogue. Final ADR sessions with Hayden Christensen, Natalie Portman, and Frank Oz were conducted in January and February 2002, when Lucas and McCallum returned to England one last time for the scoring of the film with composer John Williams and some additional shooting at Elstree Studios.

Ⓟ reparations for scoring had actually taken place the previous September, when Lucas and Williams met for a series of "spotting" sessions. Spotting entailed the pair going through the film scene by scene. Williams took notes as Lucas explained, for each scene, what he wanted the music to convey—sadness and longing, fun and adventure, military might, et cetera. With those general guidelines from which to work, Williams spent the following two to three months composing the score, reuniting with Lucas, McCallum, and the London Symphony

Orchestra in January to record it at the legendary Abbey Road Studios.

The score was recorded in two sessions per day, over a period of thirteen days, with Williams conducting the orchestra in the main hall as Lucas and McCallum listened from the sound booth or from an adjacent balcony, which Abbey Road had only recently built. "It allowed us to hear the orchestra live," Rick McCallum noted, "rather than through speakers, which was fabulous."

A simultaneous projection of the movie also let the filmmakers, for the first time, hear the score against the visual images on screen. "The first time we hear the music to picture, it is always a bit shocking," McCallum said, "because, up until that time, we've been using a temp track made up of appropriate music from other movies. We become accustomed to seeing and hearing the movie that way, with that temporary music—and suddenly, the music is all new and all

Much of ILM's postproduction work involved shooting miniatures, such as those for Dexter's Diner street exterior (above). Generic passersby were shot outdoors at ILM, walking on a bluescreen carpet (middle); then those elements were added to the diner street miniatures to create the final shot (below).

different. But it is always wonderful, because John Williams is fantastic. You get to see the film really cement itself, once the music is there. Music is the glue that holds all of it together." Working from comments and suggestions made by Lucas during the recording process, Williams continued to tweak the score in the evenings, composing on a grand piano in his hotel suite.

L ater in postproduction, the recorded score was integrated with the film's sound mix, as were sound effects, such as hot rod engine roars for the airspeeder chase. "We had a whole team devoted to sound-effects editing," Matt Wood said. "We would take a look at

a scene and basically start from scratch, as if no sound was there, and build it up layer by layer. I'd go out and record sound effects, give them to Ben Burtt, who would design them in a way that was appropriate for the scene, and that would be given to sound editors to be added in sync with the picture. About ninety-nine percent of the soundtrack was re-created in that way, after the fact."

George Lucas and Rick McCallum are visiting ILM today, just as they have done twice a week for the past several months. Their purpose is to sit down with key ILM personnel and review dailies—the most current completed, or nearly completed, visual effects shots.

Its inauspicious exterior—a series of unremarkable structures consuming a city block—do not hint at the extraordinary body of work that has been produced at ILM, but the interior décor of this particular building does. Matte paintings, photographs, and models from previous ILM projects adorn the walls leading to the screening room where Lucas and McCallum will view today's dailies. Significant equipment is also on display—notably, the Howard Anderson

optical printer, which served as the visual effects workhorse for *Star Wars: A New Hope*.

Inside the theater, stadium seating provides comfortable, unblocked views of a very large screen, showing images run from ILM's HD server and through Texas Instrument's DLP digital cinema projector by assistant editor Jim Milton. In a corner of the room, an R2-D2 unit resides next to a totem pole–like listing of all the films for which ILM has either been nominated or received an Oscar for best visual effects, starting with *Star Wars* at

the bottom, and rising through *Raiders of the Lost Ark*, *E.T.* and *Terminator 2*, and finally up to 2001's nominees, *A.I.: Artificial Intelligence* and *Pearl Harbor*.

Lucas takes a seat in the second row—flanked by visual effects supervisors John Knoll, Pablo Helman and Ben Snow, and animation director Rob Coleman—while McCallum settles himself in the front row. Also present are concept design supervisors Erik Tiemens and Ryan Church, previsualization/effects supervisor Dan Gregoire, high-definition supervisor Fred Meyer, visual effects executive producer Judith Weaver, and visual effects producers Jill Brooks, Gretchen Libby, and Heather Macdonald.

Each unit's shots are screened for Lucas, who will give them "final" approved status or ask for additional refinements. A shot from the Senate sequence has Mace Windu passing a Blue Guard, who bows; Lucas asks if there's a take in which the Blue Guard *doesn't* bow. He is assured that there is, so that shot will be reworked. In another shot in Dooku's hangar on Geonosis, the Count sends a column crashing toward the fallen Anakin and Obi-Wan. Lucas requests that the shot be cropped to bring the audience closer to the drama and asks that the two Jedi be placed more squarely under the digitally rendered column to enhance the sense of danger.

A shot of Yoda within a Republic gunship evokes laughter from the group, due to his incomplete hair effects, which make the Jedi Master's gray wisps dance around his head, fairylike. "He's using the Force to brush his hair," someone says.

During one sequence of clone troopers advancing through thick smoke with blasters firing and multicolored enemy flak bursting and streaking by them, Lucas exclaims, "Now *that's* the Clone Wars!"

(Above) **McCallum and Jim Morris, president of Industrial Light & Magic.**
(Below) **A final effects shot from the Clone War sequence includes not only computer-generated clone troopers, but ambient dust—created through ILM's in-house program—and animated laser fire.**

211

Up until a few years ago, it would've been impossible to add a scene like the one shown here late in production, as it would've entailed the expensive and time-consuming construction of an entire set. Recent technological innovations, however, made it possible to shoot Jackson alone against a bluescreen and then to add everything else afterward, from the digital set and characters to a new shadow for Mace to go with the digitally created floor material.

Anatomy of a visual effects shot: The sequence in which C-3PO is caught on the droid factory assembly line began with a wire-frame version of the character composited into a low-resolution, roughed-out version of the surrounding environment (below); the digital factory set is built up in layers to ease the burden of unduly long rendering times (top right); the finished C-3PO model in the factory geometry; the final shot is sweetened with lighting and steam effects (middle, opposite).

T he film continued to evolve after production's return from the January shoot and scoring sessions, with Lucas and Burtt adding new material and deleting extraneous material. Each of the cuts was more refined than the one preceding it, featuring fewer animatics or videomatics placeholders and more completed visual-effects shots. Even more so than in Episode I, nearly every shot in the new movie was, technically speaking, a visual-effects shot.

"Even small live-action scenes, like Padmé and Anakin sitting in front of the fire, were manipulated in some way through visual effects," Ben Burtt noted. "For example, if George didn't like the composition of a shot, we'd blow it up ten percent and shift it to the left of frame, or put a little zoom on it that wasn't originally there. We found that we could enlarge the high-definition images considerably and get much better results than we ever could with film. On film, you can't blow something up more than seventeen percent; but with these images, we could blow them up *one hundred percent*, and they would retain their quality. That enabled George to reframe, reposition, and recompose every shot if he wanted to."

In some instances, Lucas took a character out of one take and put him in another as a means of getting the best performance out of both actors in a scene. "An editor used to be stuck with either take one, take two, and so on," Burtt commented. "This time, if there was something from take three that George liked, but he didn't like what the

other actor in that take was doing, we could cut them out and put them together in a whole new, manufactured take. George experimented and moved things around until he was happy with every aspect of a shot."

Far more complex than these on-the-fly fixes executed on the Avid were the two-thousand-plus full-blown visual-effects shots generated by ILM in a two-year production period that had started a few weeks prior to principal photography, ending just weeks before the film's release on May 16, 2002. During that time, visual-effects supervisors John Knoll, Pablo Helman, Ben Snow, and Dennis Muren, along with animation director Rob Coleman and hundreds of visual- and digital-effects artists, dedicated themselves to the task, basing their fully realized shots on the previously produced animatics of David Dozoretz and Dan Gregoire and their team, as well as on digital paintings by Erik Tiemens and Ryan Church.

"The animatics not only helped us on the set," Rick McCallum remarked, "giving the cast and crew an idea of what final shots would look like, they were also something concrete we could give to ILM. The animatics were clear and couldn't be misinterpreted: 'This is a three-second

Not final animation - For animatic purposes Only

Not final animation - For animatic purposes Only

216

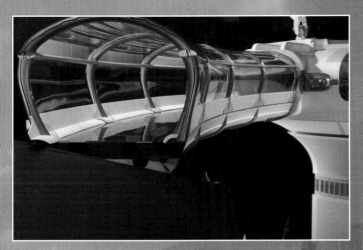

For the
tour of the cloning
facilities on Kamino,
bluescreen footage of Ewan
McGregor was composited with

Early stages of the reek battle in the execution arena. A shaded version of the model (below) enabled animators to move the creature without dealing with a cumbersome and slow high-resolution model. Live-action elements were shot with the actors on a blue-screen stage (left). Elements were added (opposite: top, middle) until the final image was realized (bottom).

218

shot with handles of eight frames on each side, a fifteen-millimeter lens, six feet off the ground—reproduce this.' It cut through a lot of misunderstanding. The animatics—as well as having the film already in a digital format—saved a lot of time and money on the visual effects."

Wasting time and money has never been Lucas's style. In fact, although the effects were crucial, providing a major-ity of the film's environments and many of its supporting characters, the director had little interest in overtaxing time and resources to achieve effects that were pristine. "I'm a strong proponent, for better or worse, of making a film that works," Lucas said. "I want the audience to be entertained by the film, moved by the film, educated by the film—but I'm not all that interested in having it be technically perfect, because technical perfection has nothing to do with telling a story.

"The original *Star Wars* was a joke, technically," Lucas commented. "I had to make a movie that normally would have cost ten times what it finally cost, and so I had to cut corners and cheat and make it kind of fuzzy so you couldn't see what was going on. In addition, most of what we did on *Star Wars*, in technical terms, had never been done before. It was all prototype stuff and, consequently, it wasn't very good. But *Star Wars* still worked as a story, and that was

what I cared about. Same with this movie. As long as the effects were good enough that people wouldn't be aware of technical flaws or inadequacies, then the story was being told. As long as it didn't interfere with the story, it was good enough for me."

The sheer size of that story, which will encompass six feature length films and more than twelve hours of screen time when it finally reaches fruition, has never been attempted by a filmmaker. Lucas is well aware of the pitfalls inherent in telling so large a tale, each chapter of which has to resonate with its predecessors *and* its successors.

"It's very difficult to tell a larger story," Lucas admitted, "and to make sure that each separate part of that story reverberates with the whole. One of the ways I've done that with Episode I and Episode II was to create scenes that were reminiscent of those in the first trilogy. Situations are the same, but with slightly different circumstances. I compare it to a musical motif, where the same themes keep recurring."

Like all the Star Wars chapters, however, this movie also has to stand on its own, establishing a unique and distinguishable tone. "Episodes IV, V, and VI were jaunty, lighthearted movies," Lucas remarked, "because that was the mood I was in at the time, and that

was the kind of story I wanted to tell. But I always knew there was a very dark backstory behind those movies, and the telling of that darker story is what we're doing with Episodes I, II, and III. If you were to sit down and watch all three of these movies at one time, you'd see that the story moves from innocence in Episode I to a very dark place in Episode III.

"And Episode II was the movie that had to get me from one to the other, so it had to have just the right tone—and I think we found that tone. It has a certain melancholy about it, but it's fun at the same time. And it appears to be a nice movie with a somewhat happy ending, at least with Anakin and Padmé. It's only when you put it in the context of the bigger story that you see the handwriting on the wall. You notice flaws in Anakin's personality that are going to sink him in the end. In this movie, you see just the beginnings of that, but it won't really come to the forefront until the next episode."

With the release of *Star Wars*: Episode II *Attack of the Clones*, Lucas and his many collaborators are only one film away from completing an epic mythological tale that has stirred the imaginations of three generations of movie-goers—most especially the imaginations of preadolescent boys, the core audience for *Star Wars*.

"George knows that world of eight-to twelve-year-old boys," Rick McCallum concluded. "Despite all the wealth and power, despite the jet stream that he inhabits, what makes George unique is that his point of view is that of a child's. That's how he sees the world. He's open and naive and youthful and curious, and he holds all of those things dear. They are sacrosanct to him. It is just who he is. Everyone else grows out of that period, and George, of course, has grown out of it at one level—but his whole essence is still in that place.

"And that, more than anything else, is the secret to *Star Wars*."

Directed by GEORGE LUCAS

Screenplay by GEORGE LUCAS and JONATHAN HALES

Story by GEORGE LUCAS

Produced by RICK McCALLUM

Director of Photography DAVID TATTERSALL, B.S.C.

Production Designer GAVIN BOCQUET

Editor and Sound Designer BEN BURTT

Costume Designer TRISHA BIGGAR

Casting by ROBIN GURLAND

Music by JOHN WILLIAMS

starring

EWAN McGREGOR

NATALIE PORTMAN

HAYDEN CHRISTENSEN

and FRANK OZ as Yoda

Co-Starring

IAN McDIARMID	PERNILLA AUGUST	AHMED BEST	OLIVER FORD DAVIES	TEMUERA MORRISON
ANTHONY DANIELS	SILAS CARSON	KENNY BAKER		

with SAMUEL L. JACKSON as Mace Windu

and CHRISTOPHER LEE as Count Dooku

Visual Effects Supervisors
JOHN KNOLL
PABLO HELMAN   BEN SNOW   DENNIS MUREN A.S.C.

Animation Director ROB COLEMAN

Concept Design Supervisors
DOUG CHIANG
ERIK TIEMENS   RYAN CHURCH

Production Supervisor STEPHEN JONES

First Assistant Director JAMES McTEIGUE

Second Assistant Director CLAIRE RICHARDSON
Second Second Assistant Director PAUL SULLIVAN

High Definition Supervisor FRED MEYERS

220

cast

Obi-Wan Kenobi	EWAN McGREGOR
Padmé	NATALIE PORTMAN
Anakin Skywalker	HAYDEN CHRISTENSEN
Count Dooku	CHRISTOPHER LEE
Mace Windu	SAMUEL L. JACKSON
Yoda	FRANK OZ
Supreme Chancellor Palpatine	IAN McDIARMID
Shmi Skywalker	PERNILLA AUGUST
Jango Fett	TEMUERA MORRISON
Senator Bail Organa	JIMMY SMITS
Cliegg Lars	JACK THOMPSON
Zam Wesell	LEEANNA WALSMAN
Jar Jar Binks	AHMED BEST
Dormé	ROSE BYRNE
Sio Bibble	OLIVER FORD DAVIES
Dexter Jettster	RONALD FALK
Captain Typho	JAY LAGA'AIA
Watto	ANDREW SECOMBE
C-3PO	ANTHONY DANIELS
Ki-Adi-Mundi & Nute Gunray	SILAS CARSON
Queen Jamillia	AYESHA DHARKER
Boba Fett	DANIEL LOGAN
Owen Lars	JOEL EDGERTON
Beru	BONNIE MAREE PIESSE
Voice of Lama Su	ANTHONY PHELAN
Voice of Taun We	RENA OWEN
Madame Jocasta Nu	ALETHEA McGRATH
Hermione Bagwa	SUSIE PORTER
Elan Sleazebaggano	MATT DORAN
Lott Dod	ALAN RUSCOE
Plo Koon	MATT SLOAN
Cordé	VERONICA SEGURA
Mas Amedda	DAVID BOWERS
Naboo Lieutenant	STEVE JOHN SHEPHERD
Clone Trooper	BODIE 'TIHOI' TAYLOR
Senator Orn Free Taa	MATT ROWAN
Senator Ask Aak	STEVEN BOYLE
Kit Fisto	ZACHARIAH JENSEN
J.K.Burtola	ALEX KNOLL
Mari Amithest	PHOEBE YIAMKIATI
R2-D2	KENNY BAKER
Oppo Rancisis	JEROME BLAKE
Eeth Koth	HASSANI SHAPI
Adi Gallia	GIN
Saesee Tiin	KHAN BONFILS
Even Piell	MICHAELA COTTRELL
Depa Billaba	DIPIKA O'NEILL JOTI

Supervising Art Director	PETER RUSSELL	Art Department Supervisor	FAY DAVID
Art Directors	JONATHAN LEE	Concept Artists	IAIN McCAIG
	IAN GRACIE		DERMOT POWER
	PHIL HARVEY		JAY SHUSTER
	MICHELLE McGAHEY		ED NATIVIDAD
	FRED HOLE		MARC GABBANA
Assistant Art Directors	JACINTA LEONG		KURT KAUFMAN
	CLIVE MEMMOTT		PHIL SHEARER
Art Department Coordinator	COLETTE BIRRELL		RAVI BANSAL
Draftspeople	ANDREW POWELL	Storyboard Artists	MARK SEXTON
	EDWARD COTTON		RODOLFO DAMAGGIO
	PETER MILTON	Sculptor	TONY LEES
	DAMIEN DREW	Concept Sculptors	ROBERT E. BARNES
Junior Draftspeople	MARK BARTHOLOMEW		MICHAEL PATRICK MURNANE
	ANDREW CHAN		TONY McVEY
	CINDI KNAPTON	Concept Model Makers	JOHN GOODSON
	PAUL OCOLISAN		JOHN DUNCAN
Set Model Makers	BEN COLLINS		CAROL BAUMAN
	KERRYANNE JENSEN		R. KIM SMITH
	MICHAEL KELM	Art Department Assistants	BETHWYN GARSWOOD
Conceptual Researcher	DAVID CRAIG		RYAN MENDOZA
Graphics/3D Modeller	PHENG SISOPHA		ROEL ROBLES
Art Department Runners	RODERICK ENGLAND		MATTHEW SAXON
	CHRIS PENN		MICHAEL SMALE

Pre-Visualization/Effects Supervisors   DANIEL D. GREGOIRE & DAVID DOZORETZ

Pre-Visualization/Effects Artists

EUISUNG LEE	BRADLEY ALEXANDER	ROBERT KINKEAD
PAUL TOPOLOS	RAYMOND WONG	SIMON DUNSDON
BRIAN CHRISTIAN	BRIAN POHL	GARY LEE
	KATIE COLE	

Stunt Coordinator/Swordmaster   NICK GILLARD

Assistant Stunt Coordinator	RICHARD BOUÉ	Dooku Stunt Double	KYLE ROWLING
Obi-Wan Stunt Double	NASH EDGERTON	Padmé Stunt Doubles	GILL STRATHAM
Jango Stunt Double	SCOTT McLEAN		CARLY HARROP

Stunt Performers

DANIEL STEVENS	DEAN GOULD	JON HEANEY
AVRIL WYNNE	DAR DAVIES	RAY ANTHONY
CHRIS MITCHELL	ROBERT SIMPER	JOSS GOWER

Production Manager (Tunisia)	PETER HESLOP	Extras Casting	MAURA FAY
Script Supervisor	JAYNE-ANN TENGGREN		ROS BREDEN
Unit Manager	TIC CARROLL	Casting Assistant	VANESSA SULMAN
Production Coordinators	PAUL RANFORD	Artists' Assistants	JILL GOLDBERG
	ISOBEL THOMAS		LEONARD THOMAS
	ANNA HALL		CHLOE MOSS
Assistant Production Coordinators	JACQUELINE KING		ALICE LANAGAN
	POLLY LEACH	Third Assistant Director	GORDON WESTMAN
Executive Assistants to George Lucas	JANE BAY	Set PA	SAM SMITH
	SARITA PATEL	Production Assistants	ALI KESHAVJI
Assistant to George Lucas	ANNE MERRIFIELD		FELICITY GIBBINS
Australian Assistant to Rick McCallum	JACQUI LOUEZ	Production Runners	JOSHUA WATKINS
US Assistants to Rick McCallum	ARDEES RABANG JUNDIS		TIM LION
	ALVIN LOPEZ	Safety Supervisor	SOTIRI SOTIROPOULOS
IT Manager	PAUL MATWIY	Security	GEORGE HATSATOURIS
Network Manager	PETER HRICAK		GAY COBHAM
Unit Nurse	JACQUIE ROBERTSON	Construction Nurse	MARGUERITTE O'SULLIVAN

222

Visual Effects Conceptual Artists

CHRISTIAN ALZMANN	MICHAEL BRUNSFELD	WARREN FU	PHILIP METSCHAN	WILSON TANG

Visual Effects Editorial and Imaging Services Group

JEROME BAKUM	DIANE CALIVA	JOSEPH GOLDSTONE	MICHAEL HUTCHINSON	JIM MILTON
RANDY BEAN	ROB DE HAAN	CLAUDINE GOSSETT	LARS JENSVOLD	TODD MITCHELL
ROBERT BONSTIN	GEORGE GAMBETTA	LARRY HOKI	GRACE LAN	MIKE MORGAN

Video Engineering and Digital Technologies

KIPP ALDRICH	ROD BOGART	SEBASTIAN MARINO	DAVID NAHMAN-RAMOS	ARI RAPKIN
BILL ANDERSON	RUSSELL DARLING	GARY MEYER	TONY PELLE	NEIL ROBINSON
ERIC BERMENDER	DAN LARGE	MARCUS NORDENSTAM	PHIL PETERSON	MICHAEL THOMPSON

Visual Effects Production and Technical Support

AMY ALLEN	MAI DELAPA	JEFF GREBE	SCOTT MEASE	TERRANCE TORNBERG
DHYANA BRUMMEL	MATTHEW EDWARDS	IAN JENKINS	STEPHEN RIERA	AMY TREVOR
DAMIEN CARR	ROBERT GIANINO	KRISTY KING	ANTHONY RISPOLI	GORDON WITTMANN
CHRISTINE CASTELLANO	RANDY GON	KATHLEEN LYNCH	JOHN SIGURDSON	DANIEL ZIZMOR

Model Supervisor   BRIAN GERNAND

Model Makers

LAUREN ABRAMS	ROBERT EDWARDS	NELSON HALL	MICHAEL LYNCH	THOMAS PROOST
BARBARA AFFONSO	THOMAS EHLINE	AARON HAYE	RICHARD MILLER	MITCHEL ROMANAUSKI
CHARLES BAILEY	DAVID FOGLER	LOREN HILLMAN-MORGAN	DAVID MURPHY	ADAM SAVAGE
SALVATORE BELLECI	JON FOREMAN	PEGGY HRASTAR	BENJAMIN NICHOLS	ROY SUTHERLAND
NICHOLAS BOGLE	CHRISTOPHER GAW	GRANT IMAHARA	RANDY OTTENBERG	LAUREN VOGT
MARK BUCK	STEVE GAWLEY	MICHAEL JOBE	ALAN PETERSON	DANIEL WAGNER
FON DAVIS	JON GUIDINGER	VICTORIA LEWIS	LORNE PETERSON	MARK WALAS
BRYAN DEWE	NEAL HALTER	ALAN LYNCH	JUAN PRECIADO	MELANIE WALAS

Effects Directors of Photography	CARL MILLER		Gaffers	THOMAS CLOUTIER
	MARTIN ROSENBERG			RICHARD DEMOLSKI
	PATRICK SWEENEY			BRAD JERRELL
First Assistant Camera Operators	MICHAEL BIENSTOCK			TIMOTHY MORGAN
	ROBERT HILL			MICHAEL OLAGUE
	RICHARD McKAY		Key Grips	WILLIAM BARR
	DENNIS ROGERS			ROD JANUSCH
Vision Engineers	SPRAGUE ANDERSON			DAVID WATSON
	ROBERT FREY		Grip	CARL ASSMUS
	DAVID LEZYNSKI		Construction Coordinator	CRAIG MOHAGEN
	CALVIN ROBERTS		Construction	CHARLES RAY
Javva the Hutt	MICHAEL SMITH		Special Effects Supervisor	GEOFFREY HERON
Costume Supervisor	GILLIAN LIBBERT		Special Effects Technician	ROBERT CLOT

IN MEMORY OF STEVE BELL

POST PRODUCTION SOUND SERVICES PROVIDED BY
SKYWALKER SOUND
"A Division of Lucas Digital Ltd. Marin County, California"

Re-Recording Mixers	GARY RYDSTROM	ADR Recorded at	"SOUNDFIRM, SYDNEY & MELBOURNE"
	MICHAEL SEMANICK		"MANDRILL AUDIO, AUCKLAND"
RICK KLINE	"4MC, LONDON"		
Supervising Sound Editors	BEN BURTT	Foley Mixer	FRANK 'PEPE' MEREL
	MATTHEW WOOD	Foley Recordist	TRAVIS CRENSHAW
Sound Effects Editors	TERESA ECKTON	Foley Artists	DENNIE THORPE
	BRUCE LACEY		JANA VANCE
Sound Fu	CHRISTOPHER SCARABOSIO	Re-Recordists	RONALD G. ROUMAS
Dialogue/ADR Editors	MARILYN McCOPPEN		BRIAN MAGERKURTH
	STEVE SLANEC	Additional Re-Recording Mixer	GARY A. RIZZO
Foley Editors	MARY HELEN LEASMAN	Mix Technicians	JURGEN SCHARPF
	KEVIN SELLERS		KENT SPARLING
Supervising Assistant Editor	COYA ELLIOTT		JUAN PERALTA
Assistant Sound Editor	ELEANOR BEATON		BRANDON PROCTOR
Assistant Dialogue/ADR Editor	MICHAEL AXINN	Machine Room Operators	SEAN ENGLAND
Apprentice Sound Editor	DAVID ACORD		MARK PURCELL
Digital Audio Transfer Supervisor	JONATHAN GREBER	Video Services	JOHN TORRIJOS
Digital Audio Transfer	CHRISTOPHER BARRON		ED DUNKLEY
	TIM BURBY	Projectionist	SCOTT BREWER
Supervising Music Editor	KEN WANNBERG	Orchestrations	CONRAD POPE
Music Editor	PETER MYLES		EDDIE KARAM
Assistant Music Editor	STEVEN R. GALLOWAY	Music Preparation	JO ANN KANE MUSIC SERVICE
Music Recorded at	ABBEY ROAD STUDIOS	Music Librarian	MARK GRAHAM
Scoring Engineer	SHAWN MURPHY	Music Performed by	LONDON SYMPHONY ORCHESTRA
Scoring Assistants	ANDREW DUDMAN	Orchestra Leader	GORDAN NIKOLITCH
	CHRIS CLARKE	Choir	LONDON VOICES
	OWEN TAMPLIN	Chorus Director	TERRY EDWARDS
Keyboard Soloist	RANDY KERBER		

ADDITIONAL SHOOTING CREW

Production Manager	BRIAN DONOVAN	First Assistant Directors	RICHARD HEWITT
Director of Photography	GILES NUTTGENS		RICHARD WHELAN
Art Director	DAVID LEE	Second Assistant Directors	MATTHEW PENRY-DAVEY
Script Supervisor	VICTORIA CHAMBERS-PIKE		TAMANA BLEASDALE
Construction Managers	LEON APSEY	Sound Mixers	BRIAN SIMMONS
	GENE D'CRUZE		SIMON BISHOP
Production Buyer	RICHARD BULLOCK	Creature Effects Supervisor	NICK DUDMAN
Art Department Assistant	MARK SCRUTON	Prosthetic Make-Up Artists	PAUL SPATERI
Gaffer	DAVE SMITH		MARK COULIER
Best Boy	SONNY BURDIS		BARRIE GOWER
Grip	PETE MYSLOWSKI		SHAUNE HARRISON
Chargehand Propman	PETER WATSON		KATE HILL
Stand-By Propman	ALEX BOSWELL	Animatronics	CHRIS BARTON
Stand-By Carpenter	PAUL NOTT-MACAIRE		MARTIN REID
Carpenter	DENNIS BOVINGTON		TAMZINE HANKS
Rigger	EDDIE SANSOM		TOM BLAKE
Chief Make-Up Artist	PAT HAY		SIMON WILLIAMS
Costume Coordinator	JO MEASURE	Foam Latex	ANDY LEE
Production Coordinators	VIRGINIA MURRAY	Creatures Coordinator	LYN NICHOLSON
	HELEN GREGORY	Special Effects	ANY EFFECTS
Assistant Production Coordinator	VICTORIA MORGAN	Special Effects Supervisor	TOM HARRIS
Transport Captain	PHIL ALLCHIN	Senior Special Effects Technician	ALEX GURUCHARRI
Nurse	JEANIE UDALL	Special Effects Technician	BARRY WOODMAN
Director of Publicity	LYNNE HALE	Stills Photographers	LISA TOMASETTI
Publicity Assistant	LISA SHAUNESSY		GILES WESTLEY
Researchers	JO DONALDSON		PAUL TILLER
	JENNY CRAIK	Stills Photography Assistant	EVELYN ROSE
	ROBYN STANLEY	Stills & Publicity Runner	IANNA WHITE
Location Researcher	ELIZABETH TULLOCH	Image Archivist	TINA MILLS
Data Logging	LIZZIE EVES		
Transport Captain	HANS VAN BEUGE	Unit Drivers	PHIL McDONELL
Unit Drivers	DUAN KERERU		RON WYNDHAM
	DAVE SIMPKINS		
Catering by	KOLLAGE KATERING	Catering Manager	KERRY FETZER
Stand-In for Ewan McGregor	RICHARD PIKE	Stand-In for Hayden Christensen	GORDON TYLER
Stand-In for Natalie Portman	NATALIE LAWLEY		

223

ITALY SHOOT
"Production Services Provided by Mestiere Cinema, Venice, Italy"

Production Supervisor	GUIDO CERASUOLO	Location Managers	SIMONA SERAFINI
Unit Manager	ENRICO BALLARIN		FRANCO RAPA
Production Coordinator	LAURA CAPPATO	Location Runner	MARCO D'ANDOLA
Assistant Production Coordinators	MARIA NOVELLA MARTINOLI	Facilities Coordinator	MARCO 'BOBO' ZANON
	TIZIANA TORTAROLO	Set Runner	DAVID GIORGIO
Production Assistant	CLAUDIA CIMMINO	Art Director	SUSANNA CODOGNATO
Transport Captain	NICOLA ROSADA	Wardrobe Assistant	BEATRICE GIANNINI
Electrician	CRISTIANO 'GIABBA' GIAVEDONI	Accountant	CARLA ZACCHIA
Grip	WERNER BACCIU	Payroll	IVANO LEPSCKY
Cashier	BERNARDO GALLI		

TUNISIA SHOOT
"Production Services Provided by CTV Services, Tunis, Tunisia"

Production Supervisor	ABDELAZIZ BEN MLOUKA	First Assistant Director	MOEZ KAMOUN
Art Director	TAIEB JALLOULI	Production Coordinator	AMEL BECHARNIA
Assistant Art Director	ANAS TALMOUDI	Accountant	ABDALLAH BAALOUCH
Unit Managers	MEIMOUN MAHBOULI	Production Secretary	LAMIA SAIDANE
	PHILIPPA DAY	Wardrobe Supervisor	NAAMA JAZI MEJRI
Matmata Location Manager	MOUNIR HLAWET	Prop Master	MOHAMED BARGAOUI

SPAIN SHOOT
"Production Services Provided by Recce & Production Services, Seville, Spain"

Production Supervisor	PEDRO MA DE UGARTE	Wardrobe Assistant	MARIA JIMÉNEZ ALFARO
Production Managers	SARKA SULCOVA	Casting	PAZ PIÑAR
	CAROLINE BONHAM-JONES	Production Secretary	SILVIA VÁZQUEZ
Production Coordinator	ISABEL DELGADO	Production Runner	JOSE LUIS RODRIGUEZ/PUMA
Set Coordinator	MÓNICA HERNANDEZ		

Special Thanks to:

JOHN FARRAND	FONDO PER L'AMBIENTE ITALIANO	MICHAEL SMUIN
KIM WILLIAMS	"CITIES OF LENNO, GRIANTE & TREMEZZO, ITALY"	EMIRATES
STEVE SMITH	ITALIAN MINISTRY OF ART AND CULTURE	SALLY BULLOCK
ROD ALLAN	"CITY OF CASERTA, ITALY"	TOM DELMAR
JAMES BRAMLEY	"PEOPLE OF TOZEUR & MATMATA, TUNISIA "	VAN BEDIENT
TED GAGLIANO	TUNISIAN MINISTRY OF THE INTERIOR	SUSAN LEAHY
TED COSTAS	SAN PABLO DE SEVILLA AIRPORT CUSTOMS	DENNIS NOONAN
TIM SCHAFBUCH	SEVILLE POLICE	CHARLIE LEDOGAR
DAVE SCHNUELLE	SEVILLE CITY COUNCIL	CYRIL DRABINSKY
STEVE MORRIS	GMU - SEVILLE	BRIAN CLAYPOOL
VICTORIA BUCHAN	PARASOUND-HOME THEATER	RENEE RUSSO
BYRON BAY KENDO CLUB	"DIGITAL FILM LAB, COPENHAGEN"	SONY-ERICSSON
SYDNEY KENDO CLUB	BRITISH MUSICIANS UNION	LANDROVER

and a very special thanks to all the Engineers at
"SONY, ATSUGI, JAPAN"

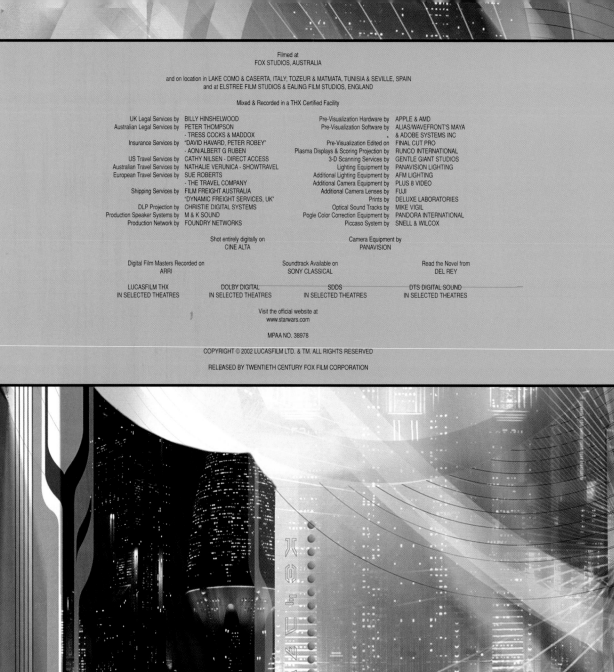

About the author

Jody Duncan has worked as a journalist covering the film industry for the past twenty years, and has authored books on the making of *Terminator 2: Judgment Day*, *Jurassic Park*, *Congo*, *Dragonheart*, *The Lost World* and *The X-Files Movie*, among others. With coauthor Laurent Bouzereau, she wrote *The Making of Star Wars*: Episode I *The Phantom Menace*. Jody also has authored dozens of articles on motion picture technology for *Cinefex* magazine, and has served as that publication's editor since 1992. Her play, *A Warring Absence*, won the national award for best original play from the American College Theater Festival in 1992.